HUMAN SOVEREIGN AUTONOMY

By Julian Hamer

Dedicated to my beautiful wife Ellen

HUMAN SOVEREIGN AUTONOMY

The Discovery of the Essential, Human Ipseity and its Establishment as the Authentic Authority of the Human Constitution.

By Julian Hamer

Contents

Introduction

1. Definitive Identification p5
2. Materialistic Exclusivity p11
3. The Insufficiency of the Present Human Mentality p15
4. Open-Hearted Sincerity p22
5. The Benchmark of Reality p25
6. Intellectual Evaluation and Feeling-Sentience p29
7. Human Ipseity p35
8. Soul Metamorphosis p41
9. Deity p47
10. The Emancipation of the Human Heart p53
11. The Condition of Reality p57
12. The Necessary Demise of Egotism p63
13. Forgiveness p69
14. The Straightforward Approach p73
15. The Heart as a Cognitive Agency p77
16. Abstractly Conceived Materialistic Philosophy p81
17. Probity, Dignity, Stature p87
18. Cognitive Estrangement p91
19. The Relinquishment of Self-centeredness p95
20. Conclusion p99
    Books by the Same Author p107

Introduction

Through the practice of immediate cognition from the perspective of the individually unique ipseity that is the crux of the human being, we further discover that the intangible yet intrinsic distinction of all other natural phenomena exists immanently. That is to say, within the condition of immediacy resides that physically elusive realm vaguely referred to as the spiritual that we here describe as the essential volume. Accordingly, within the metaphysical, essential volume lies the inherent relevance of all material conditions.

The significance of the intangible, intrinsic value of corporeal phenomena is dismissed by materialistic Western philosophy as chimerical because of a foundational, intellective prejudice that precludes inconspicuous evidence as irrational. In other words, only exclusively, physically established information is included within the materialistic world-view and consequently the value of the intangible merit of things is summarily negated.

Consequently, even though incorporeal value such as the qualitative significance that substantively distinguishes between similar phenomena, is blatantly obvious to us all through direct experience, an inequitable but generally accepted philosophy denies its existence. Furthermore a philosophical system that includes some intangibles that cannot be physically verified as admissible, while prohibiting others upon the justification of incompatible evidence, is obviously a biased abstraction that deserves the same misgiving as any other questionable doctrine.

An honest assessment of existence must dismiss the foundational premise of exclusive materialism upon the basis of its narrow and selective perspective. Clearly, in everyday life we constantly engage intangible conditions and no one seriously denies their existence. Yet, through an intellectual legerdemain, the Western way of thinking has become increasingly dominated by an excessively materialistic emphasis that is based upon an abstract formulation that is remote from actual circumstances as we directly experience them.

Thus, we recognize that materialistic Western philosophy is a speculative, abstract construct that fails to withstand empirically established knowledge. Furthermore, ominously in terms of a meaningful understanding of life, materialism is revealed to be established upon superficial parameters whereupon the appearance of things is deemed to possess significance while the substantive is conveniently overlooked.

Nonetheless, in reality the physical condition of something only veils the intrinsic merit that is the authentic significance and distinction of physical phenomena. Consequently, the essential human being becomes dissatisfied with uni-dimensionality and shallow preoccupation, and the impoverished soul yearns for intrinsic value and profoundness. Indeed, we overlook crucial value at our peril because obsession with the mere carapace of things renders life meaningless.

Consequently, the development of immediate cognition from the perspective of the intrinsic singularity of the human being may be hindered by the indirectly functioning intellect and through excessive, corporeal sensibility. Indeed, increasingly, individuality is intensely identified with the body at the detriment of the actual human host.

Therefore, the distinction between corporeal and elemental existence remains elusive to oblique rationale because essential significance is only discovered through the direct approach of the human, essential entity. Only an entity is capable of immediate engagement, while, as an adjunctive agency, the human intellectual faculty does not possess propriety differentiation and unique value but functions only obliquely through calculation and deduction. For this reason, that which must be directly encountered in order to be known remains inaccessible to even the most systematic rationale.

Through moderate discipline, the intellect is fairly easily restrained in order that an engagement between the human ipseity and a phenomenon may be directly achieved. Furthermore, the practice of immediate cognition becomes self-perpetuating by virtue of the incentive that the direct experience of the intrinsic proportion of things offers. The significance of intrinsic and qualitative value nourishes the essential human being and the direct encounter allows the human ipseity to recognize itself. In other words, the essential self discovers its own existence that thereupon becomes readily acknowledged as the sovereign identity.

Unfortunately, the established, human psyche is not so easily restrained because it has congenitally degenerated towards a state of existential anxiety and entrenched egotism. Moreover, self-circumscription inhibits the recognition of human ipseity because the uncertainty of inherent, personal value promotes defensiveness. Thus, the direct discovery and establishment of the human, singular distinction as our supreme cognitive perspective is confounded by an obsolete mentality of anxious self-preoccupation that inevitably spawns wrongdoing.

However, inherent within the fabric of existence resides a remedy of superb consequence and profound ramification. Thereby, the obsolete condition of the human psyche is transformed through an immediate concurrence with the presence of supernal goodwill. Furthermore, communion with the same definitive principle of amity is intimately and readily accessible through openhearted sincerity and the soul is thereby guided away from egocentricity through direct knowledge of existential permanence. Thereupon, the exemplary nature within the human heart remains as a constant that presents a profound, qualitative perspective towards existence and prescribes a meaningful futurity.

Through engagement with the immanent presence, we immediately experience the substantive portion of existence for ourselves, and by direct discernment of the supernal perspective, we recognize that our former egotistical mentality was founded upon an essential misapprehension. Thus, the obsolete mentality is progressively transformed through the influence of supernal goodwill as the individual progresses towards continuous, essential communion and an ever increasing realization of existential and cognitive liberty.

1. Definitive Identification

There is a significant difference between the conventional manner whereby we determine what something is, and the practice of immediate cognition from the perspective of the human ipseity. Our usual approach involves the indirect evaluation of phenomena through the intellect and by subjective perception. The intellect functions remotely from the event while feeling-sentience experientially appraises a situation, but is strongly influenced by partiality, and thereby it is selectively swayed.

The oblique, intellectual approach cannot directly encounter a phenomenon because the brain is a human faculty and not a person. It functions through evaluation and interpretation, compounding accumulated intelligence with fresh acumen. The brain, as an organ of calculation, without individual distinction, is unable to autonomously experience a situation. Explicitly, the brain is a biological instrument that must always remain subservient to a human host otherwise its purpose is rendered moot.

Subjective-sentience directly engages a situation but findings persuaded by sentiment and motivated by inclination, remain inconclusive. No matter how confident a person may be of the authenticity of their conviction, idiosyncratic perception is inadequate in terms of definitive knowledge because the subsequent intelligence remains otherwise insupportable and, consequently, indeterminate and uncertain.

The definitive identification of phenomena remains elusive to conventional cognition because the means at our disposal are inadequate through the indirect functioning of the intellect and the direct but subjective approach of respective assessment. The intellect and the capricious sentience of the human feeling nature are oblique cognitive approaches by virtue of the uncertainty of the resulting inferences. However, the significant discipline of mathematics, wherein the intellect can claim decisiveness, remains an intriguing option because deduction is the language of the intellect. Unfortunately, mathematics only concern the calculable properties of phenomena that inadequately represent the substantive entirety.

Although immediate cognition is an unfamiliar and scarcely explored cognitive approach, the direct engagement between the human, individual distinction and a phenomenon is both entirely equitable and objective. The singular distinction of the human being possesses essential ipseity and, consequently, it is able to experience things without evaluation and thereupon conclusively discover the intrinsic nature of their particular existence.

The perspective of the human, essential ipseity differs from that of subjective perception through the existential originality of the human distinction. In other words, the essential person can engage circumstances originally because it possesses explicit being, unlike the corporeal medium.

Immediate cognition may be characterized as entirely objective discernment by virtue of the directness of the encounter between the unique, intrinsic distinction of the observer, with the event. This means that a condition of immanence exists between the human, intrinsic ipseity and the quiddity of something, without the distortion of predetermination or conceptual bias.

When intellectual assessment and subjective predilection are restrained then the essential person remains uninhibited by mediation and is able to approach things straightforwardly. Through directness, the human ipseity first discovers its own unique distinction and, subsequently, immediately encounters the inherent singularity of others and the haecceity of all phenomena.

But unfamiliarity with direct apprehension and our consequent ignorance concerning our own, intrinsic identity hinders immediate cognition and we become preoccupied with a considerably inferior perspective void of substantive meaning. Remaining, is the intellectual approach that endeavors to discover conclusive evidence that, predictably, increasingly emphasizes the physical properties because those are the most concrete and readily justified.

The conventional view-point is not so much illusory as exclusionary and uni-dimensional. We observe a situation but presume prior or related knowledge concerning it and through the assumption of understanding we fail to discover the full significance. Thereby, almost everything is approached through an advocacy of interposition that obscures the original condition of things.

The full implication of something is only recognized when it is straightforwardly engaged by the human, intrinsic distinction of existence because only an entity can immediately engage a situation. The intellectual, analytical and deductive practices are ambiguous because rationale functions obliquely, and reduction only further compounds the narrowness of an abstract outlook. These things must be restrained in order that they may not distort the pristine, cognitive event.

In consequence, the unaccustomed, forthright encounter between the human ipseity and a phenomenon is an astonishingly profound event. Material conditions and physical properties appear superficial and isolated in the light of the recognition of the intrinsic distinction of things. Through the straightforward encounter inherent significance is directly apperceived because immediate cognition discerns the full dimensionality of the existence of something.

In other words, the human ipseity, as an intrinsically extant entity, engages only the similarly essential dimension of things and finds not meaning but only cursoriness in the physical condition because the material only partially represents the entirety.

Immediate cognition is an unfamiliar discipline because it requires the restraint of the conventional approaches towards knowledge. However, once the human ipseity is discovered through immediate encounter, we thereafter coordinate with our authentic distinction of existence instead of the corporeal misidentification. Thereupon, our further exploration is self-perpetuated through the enthusiasm of the discovery of the intrinsic significance of things.

The recognition of the unique ipseity that is the intrinsic distinction of the human being, is crucial to immediate cognition but once discerned, we obviously, eagerly identify with it. Subsequently, our essential uniqueness becomes sovereign and our perspective towards others all the more profound.

When the human ipseity encounters something straightforwardly the consequences are extraordinary because we recognize the intrinsic significance as well as the materially obvious. We discover that the marginal perception of conventional cognition is lamentably meager by comparison. Thereafter, the intrinsic dimension of phenomena becomes evident as the meaningful portion of the existence of things.

It would behoove us to thoroughly explore the practice of immediate engagement because therein lies cognitive autonomy. Our presumption of prior intelligence concerning existence, especially when knowledge is founded upon abstract scholarship instead of empiricism, must not be permitted to obscure serious and unprejudiced research. But the greatest hurdle of all may be the entrenched abstraction of materialistic, Western philosophy that denies substantive existence. Unfortunately, the conviction of the exclusive significance of the physical appearance and the blatantly obvious condition of things has become a fixation. Yet, without the view-point of the human, intrinsic distinction the conclusive appreciation of the entire significance of phenomena remains unattainable.

2. Materialistic Exclusivity

It is from the perspective of the human, essential identity that intrinsic significances are discovered. However, the suggested existence of human, incorporeal ipseity is directly counter to the dogma of materialistic, Western philosophy and, consequently, deliberate exploration suffers resistance and intransigence at every turn. Yet, materialism is plainly identified as a merely, abstractly conceived construct because it is established upon selective intelligence. It is a theoretical position that excludes experientially derived, intangible information on the grounds that if evidence is not physically substantiated then it cannot be justified and, consequently, it must be dismissed.

A philosophy founded upon materialistic exclusivity only corresponds obliquely to real life and fails upon practical comparison against knowledge ascertained through direct experience. Notwithstanding, we recognize through the empirical approach, a subtle volume of physically unsubstantiated reality. Thereupon, the abstractly conceived explication of existence appears inconsistent and estranged from the meaningful essential of life because it merely emphasizes the most superficial properties of phenomena. Common acquaintance severely contradicts materialism but, through intellectual persistence, the abstract construct is favorably argued and we become convinced of its merit even though it is repudiated by our own direct experience.

In fact, materialistic Western philosophy applies a sleight-of-hand whereby only the most obvious aspects of phenomena are exhaustively scrutinized and extrapolated as if they encompassed the entirety. All evidence is derived from the material condition of things while qualitative value, inherent identity and the conceptual origin of organization are dismissed as if their significance did not exist merely because essential impetus is physically elusive.

The intrinsic value of something is experientially evident through its effect even though it remains otherwise physically undetectable. Similarly, the qualitative significance of a phenomenon resists calibration and calculation and defies quantification. Yet, through astute, intellectual manipulation, those intangible values that are physically apparent through their influence, are imagined by the materialist to connote spontaneously, happenstance initiative but nothing seriously purposeful.

For example, the beauty of the human face is popularly thought to be adequately exemplified through quantification by the manner whereby it deviates from an ideal norm. If the standard of beauty is established as perfect symmetry, variations can be measured against the supposed perfect face and may be subsequently calculated and numerically represented. Thus, we establish a dry formula in place of direct experience and imagine thereby that we accurately and arithmetically delineate beauty. But it is the animated countenance that attracts interest because it indicates a vital, essential presence more significant than the frozen mask.

The quantified approach is obviously based upon the naive assumption that the symmetrical face is the most beautiful. Further, it presupposes that incremental deviation from the norm measures the degree of variance

12

between loveliness and the disagreeable countenance. However, the assumption of a standard representing beauty and the calculation of physical variation in order to evaluate it, is absurd from the empiric point of view because observation and experience clearly demonstrate that physical beauty is a qualitative value without an optimum precedent.

But the most significant failure of the attempted quantification of quality lies is the supposition that through numerical representation the entirety and the replete significance of a phenomenon is justly served. Thus, we recognize the misleading nature of the abstractly contrived approach when we compare it to the direct engagement of the circumstances themselves.

Through immediate, cognitive engagement we discover that physical appearance is merely the superficial countenance of a vastly deeper, substantive condition. In the same way that intrinsic significance is an intangible value that is only discernible through direct engagement, the essential importance of something remains elusive from the exclusively material point-of-view. While inherent significance qualitatively influences expression, essential causality that is only implied by the tangible appearance is of a more profound consequence and must be discerned through impartial cognition.

For example, the intrinsic distinction between the two Native Element Minerals, copper and silver is more significantly a qualitative one than can be discovered from a scrutiny of the physical properties. This is because the inherent disposition precedes the exterior presentation. For example, copper possesses a quality of warmth that is not apparent respecting silver even if both metals are held at exactly the same temperature.

Similarly, in terms of human manufacture, invention towards a particular purpose is not attributed to the consequence of random caprice but correctly ascribed to conceptual origin and the physical execution of an intangible idea. Yet, the materialist considers the genius of the infinitely complex natural world of compound combination towards a specific end to be the result of unimaginative, anonymous, elemental forces and exceptional coincidence.

Abstract myopia of this magnitude greatly exceeds rational justification and contradicts the scientific process upon which discipline materialistic Western philosophy is supposedly established.

The manner of thinking that sustains the logically inconsistent concept of exclusive materialism is dependent upon the fallacy whereby mechanisms, extrapolated from the abstract reduction of isolated phenomena, are thought to be universally valid. The only restraint preventing a descent into entire fiction is the periodic intrusion of common-sense.

3. The Insufficiency of the Present Human Mentality

The discovery of the human, essential distinction is not an end in itself even though the Eastern mystical schools, in search of escape and bliss, devote vast effort towards the maintenance of the experience. Although existential autonomy and immediate cognition are crucially dependent upon the establishment of our ipseity as our authentic identity, merely indulgent experience has no practical merit until our authentic identity supersedes egotism.

Typically, in the West, we overemphasize our corporeal condition and imagine that our uniqueness is physically reliant. But through immediate cognition, the human essence is able to recognize its own individual singularity and finds the encounter exhilarating. However, the significance of the human ipseity lies in its establishment as the sovereign, cognitive perspective towards other people and phenomena, and not merely as a euphoric experience of the self. Thereby, we recognize the implication of the discovery and do not merely indulge in anagogic and mystical excess.

Through immediate cognition, we discern that our essential distinction is not physically dependent and, consequently, we do not desire to escape into transcendence because we soon recognize that existence is a continuum. Therefore, we acknowledge that the value to us of the discovery of our singular uniqueness lies less in the experience itself but significantly in our further development. Obviously, it is of enormous consequence that we practice immediate cognition after the recognition of our authentic identity because the establishment of the human ipseity as our essential view-point offers the potential of the direct discovery of the meaningful priority of our everyday life.

The human, singular distinction directly engages phenomena and discovers the essential, yet intangible significance. Thereby, through immediacy, we establish a cognitive condition wherein the merit of things is found to exist inherently and significance is seen to reside not superficially but intrinsically.

The indirectly functioning, human, cognitive faculties are unable to approach the substantial existence of things because the intellect and feeling-sentience do not possess essential ipseity. Only the essential person can directly engage phenomena because the establishment of cognitive immediacy is a direct encounter without mediation or interpretation. The intellect consistently assesses and evaluates, obliquely estimating the nature of circumstances, while the feelings endeavor to subjectively appraise. But the human essential distinction always engages the similarly essential significance of phenomena through immediate engagement.

The emotional nature, however, is the vulnerable disposition and state of temper of the human constitution that is consolidated as the psyche. It resides within a condition of uncertainty and, consequently, it is egocentric and defensive by nature as a result of its sense of existential isolation, and by virtue of seeming to be mortal. Furthermore, through self-absorption, it is susceptible to all manner of adverse influences if they appear even remotely capable of assuaging its profound sense of uneasiness and existential ambivalence.

The human psyche must become reestablished upon a thoroughly meaningful footing in order that we may progress towards a condition of sovereign autonomy. Otherwise, the indisposed and susceptible nature of our emotions will hinder further human development. A self-centered disposition, adrift and unpredictable, will inevitably confound the establishment of the human ipseity as the primary, cognitive perspective because it works against the broader view.

Peace of mind may be fleetingly experienced through considerable discipline and self-restraint but will-power is only temporarily effective and, consequently, compelled emotional composure must be constantly reiterated.

The unfortunate fact of the matter is that the human being does not possess the inherent capacity of comprehensive soul-amelioration. Moreover, the mentality established through ages upon our own uncertain merits is redundant in terms of a meaningful, human future. It is an obsolete, pre-conditional paradigm that may have served us during our earlier development but now must be superseded by a new archetype.

Fortunately, a new and ultimate disposition resides immanently extant in direct relationship to the human heart, as an ever-present exemplar that can only be properly justified as authentic through personal experience. Accordingly, upon immediate engagement, we discover the essential and comprehensive assurance that the soul must have in order to become reestablished upon existential certainty. Thereupon, the redundant condition of the human psyche is superseded by a vastly superior principle that is immediately conspicuous for its exhaustive expanse of amity and goodwill. It is directly accessible as a potential that becomes realized within the heart to the degree that we identify with it and receptively allow it to recondition our innermost nature.

However, we do not have to accomplish the transformation ourselves. Indeed, we are unable to achieve effective renewal because we scarcely possess even a distant concept of the nature of the new human condition. That which we imagine as an advanced paradigm is likely to be lamentably remote from the reality. However, it is our task to diligently acquiesce to the metamorphic transformation of the soul by recognizing the distinction between our own obsolete mentality and that which we experience of the new, through immediate, openhearted sincerity.

Through the portal of a sincere heart, we directly engage a hitherto unfamiliar disposition and recognize the stark discrepancy between our own uncertain condition and that of irreproachable integrity. Thenceforth, we permit our self-centered nature to become reestablished through the pervasive influence of a new, dispositional archetype. All that is required of ourselves is sincerity and an open heart. Accordingly, we enter into an immediate intimacy with the new paradigm whereby our psyche is gradually superseded because we gratifyingly discover that the progressive condition that we engage retains nothing of the disorder of the dysfunctional mind, but it is in every respect qualitatively juxtaposed.

Thus, the human soul becomes increasingly transformed and re-founded upon amity and goodwill because it is no longer uncertain and self-centered but is securely and profoundly established upon the assurance of concord and benignity. The soul no longer hinders the progressive advancement of the human being towards sovereign autonomy but enhances its establishment through the ever-present disposition of the supernal nature.

Nothing is lost through human development according to the measure of the supernal mind, but the unsound, former complexion is effectively superseded by consummate maturation. Thus, the human being moves steadily forward towards an impressive destiny, the noble and magnanimous nature of which we can scarcely conceive.

4. Open-Hearted Sincerity

Through immediate cognition we discover the immutability of our own unique distinction because human ipseity exists in an original and extant condition as a statement of existence. The incident of human corporeality is irrelevant to ipseity because essential being is emphatic and not contingent upon circumstances. Ipseity exists in a contiguous state with the essential of all phenomena. Consequently, the human being becomes aware and explores the nature of its singular uniqueness through immediate cognition and upon the strength of direct engagement, establishes an intimate knowledge of absolute reality. Thereafter, hypothetical constructs, belief systems and abstract improvisation fail to persuade because we have immediately experienced essential reality and nothing less than directly authenticated conditions will suffice.

In possession of definitive knowledge regarding essential existence through direct concurrence, we determine the authenticity of the prospective paradigm of human nature beyond the present mentality. While the soul must, necessarily engage the ideal exemplar through open-hearted sincerity, nevertheless, having directly discerned our singular, unique distinction, we recognize the authenticity of the progressive archetype through direct knowledge of the timbre of substantive existence. In other words, we are aware of fundamental reality through immediate cognition and we have the measure of it. Thus, through open-hearted sincerity we recognize the value and significance of the immediate presence of a new architecture that is opposite to our own myopic and self-centered mentality. Comparatively, we find our former condition starkly wanting, and we yearn to identify and embody the new condition.

Ingenuousness is both an essential and sufficient basis for the inauguration of the metamorphic transformation of the soul. Clearly, are unable to transform ourselves because we do not possess the resources, entrenched as we are in an atrophied mentality that is self-defeating. If we imagine that we can change our soul through force of will and invention, the consequences will not be an authentic metamorphic revolution but merely a rearrangement of the existing condition. Consequently, is vital that we recognize and embrace our incorporeal singularity because that which transforms us is similarly essential. Yet, we do not wish to functionally improve while maintaining the same moribund psyche. Accordingly, we turn with open-hearted sincerity to the immanent presence of the new human archetype and thus steadily secure our conversion from a superficial sense of self to our authentic status.

It is essential to permit the immanent principle to enact the reconstitution of the soul because without the aegis of the new archetype itself, nothing of consequence is achievable. If we imagine that through emotional manipulation and the ratification of different ideals that we somehow may achieve an optimum mentality, we are not addressing a metamorphic transformation but merely pursuing lateral change.

However, having experienced the intangible nature of essential existence through immediate engagement from the view-point of the human ipseity, we recognize that which we engage of the new archetype through openhearted sincerity is of a qualitatively similar, existential caliber.

In terms of nature, an archetype is the quintessential arrangement and conceptual structure that comprehensively ensures the accomplishment of the metamorphic cycle of development of an organism, through alternate expression towards a very specific end. The structure of a creature or plant must conform to the ideal otherwise it ceases to be viable and subsequently disintegrates. A parallel exists in terms of the human soul when we consider the transformation of our obsolete psyche as a metamorphic translation from a previous condition into a complete and successive reinterpretation.

Archetype is a convenient word to describe the fundamental and structural disposition of the human soul but the analogy is otherwise overextended. That which occurs is a foundational realignment whereby the existential basis of the psyche ceases to rest upon its own uncertain value. Through immediate experience of the supernal exemplar within the heart, the obsolete mentality is superseded by an immanently experienced exemplary nature.

The immanent presence that is discovered through open-hearted sincerity is not a capricious elemental force but an extraordinary entity that entirely personifies wholesome goodness and all of its qualitative ramifications. Our familiarity with intrinsic, intangible existence as a benchmark of authenticity permits us to evaluate other incorporeal experiences and determine their legitimacy through qualitative comparison.

5. The Benchmark of Reality

In order to temper philosophical and religious idealism, the immediate experience of phenomena, including the recognition of the intrinsic singularity of other people, serves to moderate abstract conceptualization through an experiential background of originally ascertained knowledge. By means of the practice of direct engagement from the view-point of the human ipseity, we discover the distinction between the conjectural product of the oblique and abstract function of the intellect, and immediacy wherein the authentic condition in which the essential of things resides. Similarly, the imagination, when creativity is unsubstantiated by a direct knowledge of the authentic nature of existence, might pursue all manner of unjustified fiction were it not for the restraint of commonsense.

Commonsense is a constraint established upon practical experience. As such it is antithetical to fantasy because it offers proportion to imaginative excess. But the value of commonsense is precariously dependent upon the soundness and integrity of the origin from which it is derived, and the appropriateness of its application.

In order to navigate effectively through conjectural rationale and determine the authentic relevance of an explication, it is essential that we establish a foundation of absolute authenticity.

René Descartes (1596 – 1650), sought to constitute and justify his philosophical and religious position upon the qualitative reference of the immediate experience of the existence of his own singular distinction. Further, he endeavored to expand the justification for the significance of unique, human individuality through further thoughtful evidence. Unfortunately, he did not realize that the immediate recognition of human, incorporeal singularity is unamenable to rational qualification and that deduction cannot conclusively demonstrate the existence of incorporeal, intrinsic distinction. Ironically, to this day, the abstract logic of Descartes continues to elicit interest, while the description of his direct experience of ipseity and of the human relationship towards supernal nature is derided as mysticism.

Through the aegis of the direct, cognitive approach, intrinsic significance is found to possess inherent testimony of its own existence. Subsequently, the human ipseity becomes established as the primary cognitive perspective whereby the similarly essential value of phenomena is readily apprehended. Furthermore, immediate engagement through the perspective of the human, singular ipseity, provides access to the elemental and intrinsic condition of phenomena.

However, the intellect cannot successfully qualify or decisively justify intrinsic existence because reason functions indirectly and remotely from the actual event and essential circumstances are only implied by physical evidence. Only the intrinsic person can directly encounter phenomena and discover essential merit. Thus, we need to distinguish between our corporeal condition and our intrinsic identity because otherwise we will only be able to interpret phenomena and experiences through oblique evaluation and, inevitably, our viewpoints and opinions will remain uncertain.

Yet, to make it very clear, the human ipseity is not the same as the personality. Personality is not the authentic identity but it is the variable, characteristic manner of human expression. That is to say, the unique distinction that essentially differentiates one individual from another is not idiosyncratic but existentially constant. Personality is variable and transient, subject to alteration. But the human essence remains consistent as an emphatic statement of singular existence.

If we become preoccupied merely with an intellectual assessment of existence, we displace direct involvement with abstraction and endeavor to deduce the nature of things through rationale instead of immediate cognition. Even the most systematic and logical approach remains uncertain if it is empirically unfounded and instead conceived upon accrued consensus and obliquely premeditated scholarship. Thus, we avoid the actual circumstance and primarily trust in accumulated explication. This practice of abridged understanding, remote from the actual event, establishes a contrived and confusing, synthetic realism. This may be sufficient in terms of the myriad conflicting philosophies in circulation, but regarding scientific discipline, hypothesis that fails in application is valueless.

Nevertheless, faced with the proposition of an unfamiliar, cognitive approach, the establishment defensively resorts to precedent, the arguments of prior acumen and debate, as if a volume of persuasion were synonymous with substantiation.

Regardless, indirect approaches are constitutionally unqualified to challenge knowledge that is only discernible through immediate engagement. Furthermore, the quiddity of human existence possesses a unique perspective towards life, knowledge of which cannot be attained upon the strength of rationalization. In the end, direct cognition and oblique, abstract thinking are incommensurate practices because, as an entity, the human, essential distinction can engage phenomena directly without the intermediary of a corporeal function.

Upon the basis of knowledge achieved through an impartial encounter towards others and the immediate engagement of circumstances from the view-point of human ipseity, we establish an unshakable certainty that becomes the measure and standard against which both abstract proposition and conjecture are tried for their authenticity. Against immediately discerned reality through the authority of the human essence, the value of philosophical and religious positions is sounded for their coincidence or divergence with substantive existence.

6. Intellectual Evaluation and Feeling-Sentience

The way towards autonomous cognition is through the establishment of the human ipseity as the foundational authority and essential identity of the human constitution. The discovery of human, intrinsic singularity and the recognition of existential uniqueness, is pivotal to the attainment of conclusive discernment.

Unless that which is essentially extant and ultimately dependable becomes positioned as our cognitive perspective towards all circumstances, we cannot expect to achieve definitive knowledge because otherwise we engage phenomena from a less than certain, existential position.

It is imagined by some, that feeling-sentience somehow offers insightful intelligence. But upon closer examination, we find that information derived spontaneously and instinctively is of only very questionable value and is far from categorical. Being of mysterious and vague origin the merit of innate knowledge and premonition remains uncertain.

The air of mystery associated with precognition lends a measure of conviction because the miraculous possesses suspenseful anticipation, and fascination can be seductive. The practitioner is accorded esteem upon the strength of counterfeit wisdom merely because the recipient is ignorant of the authentic condition of things and unaware of the means of their discovery. A harmless pastime, divination is misleading if it is accorded more than casual indulgence.

Similarly, knowledge attained through deduction offers only obliquely derived intelligence concerning phenomena because of the indirect manner of the function of the intellect. Only the human ipseity can originally engage something and discover its intrinsic significance because the essential distinction of the human being necessarily engages phenomena immediately. The human entity itself is the explicit identity while the intellectual faculties and feeling-sentience offer only marginal and superficial intelligence because they cannot directly encounter phenomena. Without intrinsic significance of their own, the conventional faculties only operate as intermediary functions and, consequently, knowledge obtained indirectly is derivative and not uniquely acquired.

Through systematic deduction, the intellect is able to assess circumstances based upon the caliber of the particular intelligence with which it is working and the strength of the individual capacity of logical evaluation. In an equally ambiguous vein, feeling-sentience endeavors to evaluate by subjective sensibility as if human instinct and prescience possessed superior insight. In this way, the intellect calculates dispassionately while feeling-sentience offers only a subjective perspective. But neither approach provides definitive intelligence concerning the intrinsic condition and identity of ourselves or the substantive condition of physical phenomena.

Through the congenital inability of the intellect to immediately engage, because it is only able to function obliquely, information is ideally reduced into calculable terms in order to assist its manipulation and assessment. Thus, we find that the reducible and accountable properties of phenomena are distinctly overemphasized at the expense of intangible but pertinent evidence such as the quality and value of things. This arrives at an inevitably skewed perspective towards existence whereby the plain condition of things becomes accentuated while the intrinsic, incorporeal significance is neglected. The resultant impersonal, mechanical and mathematically contrived world-view is a starkly evident pariah of modern times.

Nevertheless, the subjective approach may judiciously discern qualitative significances while remaining unable to definitively demonstrate their deeper importance because essential quality and value exist without physical evidence and, consequently, their existential implication is overlooked. Consequently, while we know that intangible value is authentic, yet we are unable to recognize the integral significance from a material point-of-view because qualitative merit remains essentially incommensurate with calculation.

Formerly, art was the means whereby the existence of experientially recognized intangible evidence was affirmed and communicated. However, through an excessive emphasis on intellectual justification and disconnected evaluation, art has become an increasingly dilettante expression, void of significant content and, consequently, prone to vulgar, commercial exploitation. That is to say, the general acceptance of inarticulate art is a self-evident contradiction that has arisen because we have become uncertain of the existence, the value, and the significance of intangible existence.

The means whereby conclusive intelligence concerning the existential condition of phenomena is achieved is immediate cognition through the perspective of the human ipseity. Alone, the human, essential distinction engages everything straightforwardly and, as an entity, it encounters phenomena without the conventional cognitive intermediary of intellectual evaluation or feeling-sentience. It finds things in their elemental condition and identifies the intrinsic condition of their existence because, possessing emphatic continuance, it encounters everything essentially.

The authenticity of the human ipseity and the efficacy of immediate cognition cannot be intellectually determined because the nature of reason is inadequate to conclusively identify the existence of intangible significances. The intellect calculates and evaluates in a sequential, logical manner alike to mathematics but it cannot experience because it is an organic function without the virtue of essential identity. Only ipseity is able to directly engage phenomena and discover their intrinsic significance.

In other words, the intellect is incommensurate with being because it does not possess unique, individual distinction. As a corporeal organ, it merely evaluates circumstances logically and remotely. Consequently, the endorsement of deduction in matters pertaining to being is irrelevant because emphatic, intangible existence cannot be conclusively reasoned but must be directly determined.

The intellect always functions discursively and can never immediately engage something because it is not a person. A cerebral function cannot experience but must evaluate evidence after the event or imaginatively, in expectation. Only ipseity can engage phenomena directly and, consequently, immediate cognition can be justified solely through the empirical directness of the essential, human identity.

The human ipseity approaches all things straightforwardly without explication because it exists definitively. It finds things as they exist in their own right, before and irrespective of human rationale and deductive evaluation. It achieves this through immediacy, engaging phenomena straightforwardly and impartially. Thereby, it discovers the nature of the existence of things without the assistance of presupposition and requires no further qualification.

7. Human Ipseity

There is only one reality. There is only real or unreal. Conventionally, we assume that we correctly interpret existence upon the basis of the most apparent evidence but in fact we easily overlook the relevance of the intrinsic and meaningful nature of things. Yet, the physically elusive, qualitative connotation of the material condition of something epitomizes the actual connotation. Established upon the most blatant material testimony we have become convinced of the exclusive value of a partial perspective. As a result, through a shortsighted materialistic preponderance that overemphasizes the appearance and overlooks the innate nature, we assume that a cursory view represents the entirety.

If we endeavor to perceive the incorporeal but meaningful proportion of existence solely in physical terms, our understanding remains either vague and elusive, or we endeavor to find meaning through a fantastically imagined excess that supposes that physical phenomena possess a somehow rarefied essence and yet retain their original identity. It is extraordinary how the disparity of an inadequate exposition of life is frequently compensated by a fictional hypothesis.

From the exclusive material, narrow view we fail to recognize that the intrinsic significance and essential value of things reveal their inherent distinction because the existence of value is only distantly implied by the physical but it is otherwise imperceptible to conventional cognition.

Reality does not alter merely through human dissension or misconception. The consequence of a

35

distorted perspective impairs a meaningful rapport with existence but does not change reality one iota. We are the ones who are disadvantaged through the assumption of an abstractly contrived and fabricated interpretation of existence founded upon superficial appearances. Thereby, we accept the validity of a peripheral condition wherein we suppose that material substance is the full extent and exclusive significance of existence. Consequently, we dwell within the supposed parameters of a world-view that is essentially fictitious because existence is perfunctorily and incompletely assessed.

Only ipseity can engage phenomena directly, and through immediate cognition, we discover that our materialistic philosophy towards existence obscures reality because it establishes an interpretative myopia wherein we transpose everything into physical terms.

Human ipseity approaches all things straightforwardly and originally without the mediation and explication of our conventional, cognitive faculties. Deduction and feeling-sentience can never recognize the authentic nature of existence because they are inadequate to the task and an exclusively physical perspective cannot grasp the concept of an intangible and immanent portion of existence that is intrinsically of greater meaning than the appearance.

Much to the disappointment of those who enjoy maintaining a sense of mystery and subsequent superiority, there is nothing enigmatic about immediate cognition. Phenomena are engaged directly and discovered for their otherwise overlooked intrinsic significance. Through the authentic identity of the human being we discover the full dimension of the existence of things and thereby we recognize the impoverished and superficial nature of blatant appearances. While the material condition of something is obviously authentic, nonetheless, it is recognized as insufficient and frivolous when the material evidence is alleged to comprise the entirety.

Partial evidence concerning phenomena or circumstances is inevitably misleading even when it applies merely to the mundane. Materialistic Western philosophy is an erroneous perspective wherein only the outward condition of things is deemed pertinent. But it has become so severely entrenched as the customary bias upon which we evaluate life, that we have come to deny our own experiences to the contrary. Thereby, the intrinsic significance of things, including human, unique and intangible singularity, is thought void of pertinence merely because it is not physical. Consequently, essential value and intrinsic relevance are overlooked, and our perspective encourages and maintains a bias of superficiality and meaninglessness.

By maligning human inherent, incorporeal uniqueness and presupposing that our identity is entirely physical, our progress towards cognitive autonomy is severely obstructed. Denied original significance, our innate cognitive ability to directly engage the elemental nature of things is impaired. By excluding the importance and implication of human, incorporeal ipseity we fail to recognize the immanent nature of essential existence and instead we invent substitute realms of parallel dimensions or ethereal physicality, in order to explain away the contradiction between an abstractly conceived philosophy and our everyday, inconsistent experience of intangible significances.

Furthermore, the extension of materialistic, Western philosophy by academic authority, adversely compounds the human malaise of existential uncertainty and encourages the inverse religiosity of atheism. If we imagine ourselves to be merely physical, then we must also be thoroughly mortal and, consequently, the continuum of human existence, recognized through the immediate cognition of ipseity, is obscured and we institute conditions upon ourselves that are essentially untenable. We find ourselves in a spurious, self-imposed mental state that is entirely against our own interests and impedes our progress towards self-determination.

The human ipseity exists irrespectively of physical circumstances, and everyone possesses unique and individual distinction which is the authentic, human identity. But we are suspicious of intangible existence because we have come to believe that the physical alone is substantial. Yet if we turn our attention to those things that we know to exist without physical representation, such as quality, value, and inherent identity, we begin to realize that the profound proportion of things lies not in the material condition but intrinsically and intangibly.

When we look at another person from the perspective of our own uniqueness, we cannot fail to recognize their own inherent and singular status. Furthermore, we discover that human, intrinsic significance and inherent identity is not corporeally apparent and that there exists a distinction between the appearance and the essence. Indeed, while the appearance anchors our attention, nevertheless we find the material to be superficial when juxtaposed to the singular, essential identity.

The dynamic whereby we recognize the substantive nature of another person or phenomena, is immediate cognition. We cannot discover the intrinsic substance of things by conventional perception. They must be engaged directly from the perspective of the human ipseity.

Everyone possesses unique and singular, incorporeal distinction. When the human ipseity recognizes itself through immediate cognition, it finds that it resides independently from physical circumstances. Moreover, essential significances exist in a condition of immanence concerning the relationship to the essential of everything else, and they are only separately discerned by their qualitative inherence.

Immanence is the state in which crucial significances reside and through the direct engagement of an impartial mind, we discover the particular, qualitative distinction of something that epitomizes its identity.

8. Soul Metamorphosis

The manner whereby the human soul may advance towards the recognition of individual, essential significance, and subsequently, cognitive autonomy, significantly involves the realization of existential uniqueness. But, simultaneously, the condition of the human heart must be addressed because, otherwise, it will distort authentic experience. The human soul is the crux of the human constitution wherein the quality of the individual disposition is conceived.

In order to discern the qualitative distinction that intrinsically differentiates between phenomena, it is vital to engage things directly. Further, it is the human, essential principle itself that must immediately encounter phenomena in order that the substantive significance of something may be discovered. Thereupon, through immediate cognition, we determine the full dimensionality of the existence of phenomena. But when egotism intrudes, we are distracted by myriad insecurities and an uncertain sense of self-pollutes the sapient view. In other words, emotional dysfunction engenders defective understanding and intrudes upon insightfulness.

Naturally we are each flawed in our own way, but through openhearted sincerity towards the immanent presence, we initiate a corrective process of soul reestablishment.

While the crucial objective for the human soul is the realization and application of singular existential and cognitive autonomy, when a redundant mentality contaminates immediate cognition, the most effective resource concerns turning our attention towards the

41

exemplification of a sound mind that resides contiguously to the individual heart.

Thereby the obsolete state of self-centeredness is transformed inside out and a new integrity is steadily installed at the foundation of the human psyche. In other words, the heart may be transformed by supernal influence to the degree that the soul selects between the former, redundant mentality, and the directly engaged, exemplary disposition.

Those who pretend to have accomplished a spiritual state of virtue and superiority err significantly if they fail to avail themselves of the above described metamorphic dynamic. The human soul is not lastingly transformed by any other means because the establishment of a successive disposition requires sincere open-heartedness and existential vulnerability which is something egotism cannot abide.

But the consequences of immediate concurrence with the supernal exemplar are a complete reorientation from ego-defensiveness to sanity and from a false sense of self to our authentic distinction. No one would choose the lesser and ignoble conceit of egotism upon a glimpse of our potential and destined liberty. But the transformation itself is not ours to perform.

Human advancement is neither mysterious nor complicated, but it requires a profound reestablishment of identity. If we imagine that human origin is merely capricious and that our significance is essentially corporeal then we obstruct the qualitative evolution of the soul.

Similarly, if we assume that we can transform our redundant human psyche through will-power relying upon our short-sighted, human capacities, we are severely mistaken. In order to introduce an entirely antithetical mentality, it is essential that a metamorphic transformation of inconceivable proportions and profundity take place. The capacity to conclude such a conversion does not reside within human capability.

Nevertheless, the transformation of the human mentality is achievable without our genius, although individual initiation remains prerequisite. In other words, without human instigation the heart-of-the-soul remains closed to the transformative presence of the supernal nature. Yet, through sincere openheartedness, the innermost psychology is prepared and inclined towards rectification. Thereupon, transformation occurs instantaneously at every moment when we discover through an attentive conscience, a dissonance of disposition. Earnestly and expectantly, we open and extend the heart towards worthy reorientation.

The onus is not upon us to effect a change of psyche because we cannot achieve metamorphic restructuring while we are ignorant of the constitution of a successive standard. We might affect behavioral alteration through will-power, but this is a difficult task that would require incredible discipline in order to establish a healthy mentality. But even if self-initiated amelioration were attainable, the foundation of the human disposition would, nevertheless, remain uncertainly established. Indeed, the consequences of autogenous refinement are bound to be inadequate because they are conceived and systematized through the efforts of an inadequate mind.

What occurs through open-hearted sincerity is the relinquishment of an obsolete disposition and the ready accommodation of profound restructuring upon an entirely different basis than formerly. The act of turning the heart towards the immanent exemplar is itself profound and inaugural of reorientation because we thereby select improvement over our shortcomings. Through openhearted sincerity, engagement with the supernal nature becomes immediate and establishes itself as a new foundation of certitude and benignity that resolves the human plight.

The supernal exemplar that we wish to establish within our own soul as the foundational premise of our disposition, is not material but immanent and qualitative. Through direct cognition, we already recognize the nature of immediacy and we know that the essential distinction of things exists instantly. The successive nature occupies the same condition, that is why the new human, constitutional paradigm is consistently and persistently accessible to every human soul.

It is unfortunate that this essential and necessary dynamic of a transformation is not straightforwardly grasped but remains concealed through human misconstruction and artifice. Thus, we find that the exercise of open-hearted sincerity has become tarnished through much foolish connotation and appears to the modern majority to be something self-deceptive and religiously contrived. Similarly, the concept of a supernal, exemplary disposition that exists without spatial representation, is abhorrent to our materialistically exclusive perspective. Consequently, either the whole concept of metamorphic renewal is ridiculed as pretentious and self-righteous, or it is embellished beyond recognition as a dogma, only to be innocently swallowed by the sincere but unsuspecting aspirant.

The soul must relinquish the old mentality and identify with the successive disposition because there is no meaningful future under the existing mindset. Fortunately, regeneration is an individual and intimate assignment and a sincere heart will readily discover the supernal paradigm that is contiguously positioned within the human constitution.

The human soul engages and identifies with immanent presence of goodwill and amity through the heart. The heart is the epitome of the soul. It is essential and, consequently, it is no more described by the physical organ than the human ipseity is characterized by the brain. In order that the soul may become reestablished upon a righteous foundation, the heart must become receptive to an unconventional paradigm that is quite unlike its former egocentricity.

We cannot realistically conceive or imagine our subsequent condition because we have to grow into it through rendering the heart susceptible to a new paradigm. While we are thoroughly familiar with the existing mentality and the inevitable ramifications of human dysfunction, the successive nature is qualitatively, entirely juxtaposed and unconceivable from our present, marginal perspective towards existence.

9. Deity

The human concept of deity is inevitably naive, as a long and despicable history of holy war and cruelty under the banner of god, has abundantly demonstrated. Obviously, foreknowledge concerning a deity is an abstraction in much the same way as a pre-conceptual assumption concerning any phenomena obscures immediate cognition. Typically, our notions of the divine range wildly from a supreme, autocratic despot, to the capricious potentate with occult power that can be swayed and persuaded to serve our every whim. Alternatively, there remains the archaic notion of an unreasonable godhead that demands virtue of us while having apparently instilled sinfulness as our essential foundation.

Whatever shade of divine sanctimony a person may choose to endorse, a human concept of something entirely mysterious and without reasonable reference will inevitably lack credible authority. Obviously, popular doctrine is propagated more by hearsay than actual knowledge, and in the same manner that we harbor abstract concepts concerning any subject, we hinder realistic understanding through conceptual predilection. Indeed, in the manner of immediate cognition, it is crucial that we approach the supernal ethos discovered within the heart, with an entirely impartial mind. Thereby, assuming ignorance, we build upon originally derived knowledge in order that we may discover the authentic condition of the object of our interest.

Consequently, through immediate engagement from the perspective of an impartial mind, we encounter circumstances without preconception or precedent. For example, if we meet another human being we judiciously set aside what we imagine we know of them from their physical appearance, and thereby we discern their singular uniqueness.

That is to say, we do not recognize the singular distinction of something if we approach phenomena with apparent foreknowledge or anticipation. It is the same with a deity. In reality, we have no adequate concept of the divine, but we have merely amassed a considerable volume of circumstantial evidence upon the basis of which we have subsequently established a breadth of purported understanding that is inevitably remote from reality. Some of those conclusions are blatantly fictional while the more convincing yet remain circumstantially derived and impossible to verify.

However, through immediate cognition, the human ipseity, without contingency or precondition, is able to directly discern the intangible significance of all phenomena. The physical appearance of something serves to anchor our attention but it is the human essence itself that discovers the intrinsic value. However, a deity must be approached from a different perspective because we lack the advantage of a physical frame of reference. In this case, it is through openhearted sincerity that the individual approaches the supernal, and it is within the soul that the event of communion takes place.

In this way we discover that a deity does not require a definition, but conversely, our knowledge rests upon the direct experience of the qualitative distinction and inherent nature that we discern through immediate engagement. It is to this entity that we turn through open-hearted sincerity when we become alert through conscience and disquiet of the inevitable shortcomings and consequences of existential misidentification. It is this same entity that becomes established as the new and unblemished foundational nature of the human soul through our persistent overture and willing consent.

Thereupon, our increasing familiarity profoundly changes our disposition because we become assured, and subsequently, we cease to function from the former mentality that failed us, and we come to increasingly exemplify an extraordinary, successive nature.

Prior knowledge concerning a deity is not required because our experience is original and unprecedented. Presumption and preconception are entirely a hindrance to immediate experience because they distort the straightforward approach. We do not need to know anything concerning the godhead and if we imagine that we do, we are severely mistaken and only obstruct our own advancement. Yet, through openhearted sincerity, we are able to establish a certitude against which all doctrines and assertions may be evaluated and tried for their authenticity.

Emancipation from an obsolete condition of soul motivated by existential uncertainty and subsequent, defensive egotism, is unattainable through human artifice. Yet, the new condition exists, as it were, concurrently with our redundant disposition, but it is always approachable through open-hearted sincerity. Thereupon we find that the exemplary disposition becomes increasingly distinct to the degree that the soul identifies with the successive instead of our former, obsolete nature.

The transformation of the soul is neither mystical nor enigmatic. A new endowment exists in immediate proximity as a pragmatic and essential necessity. A quick look at the lamentable consequences of human derangement readily justifies the urgency.

However, obviously, we do not possess the new disposition as a constitutional or inherent fait-accompli but it increases within the human psyche through our personal determination. Upon immediate concurrence within a receptive heart, we directly experience the supernal exemplar and thereby inaugurate a transformation towards an entirely refashioned nature.

Assuming absolutely nothing, through open-hearted sincerity we initiate and steadily experience a fundamental alteration of manner from a self-circumscribed and restrictive perspective to noble maturity. We restrain our busy intellect with its myriad conceptual assumptions and permit the supernal nature to be to us, whatever it is in reality.

We recognize that mere belief without the test of application is insufficient and if we are determined to know the authenticity of a position, we explore it pragmatically. Without personal experience we may be swayed by any deviously fabricated doctrinal structure, well postulated and persuasively argued perhaps, but otherwise without merit.

But through our own, direct experience we discover the timbre of authenticity and we recognize that the transformation of our disposition from self-centeredness and insecurity is initiated through sincerity and not pharisaic sanctimony. We require no intermediary because the transformation of the soul is an entirely personal process. Furthermore, in terms of the ingenuous heart, cognition from the perspective of sincerity is our ultimate barometer of legitimacy.

Concurrence with the supernal exemplar through openhearted sincerity, allows the individual to relinquish control. A stark perspective is evident. Our engagement is of such a quality that any presumption of authority is counterproductively inappropriate. Consequently, we recognize another dimension of the dynamic of soul transformation. We find ourselves distasteful of our cheerless disposition and yearn to be of the quality of the supernal. A powerful determination arises, that buoys our determination that might otherwise flounder through discouragement, and we abandon control to a vaster wisdom than we can imagine.

The discrepancy between the disquiet and uncertainty founded upon an isolated and mediocre sense of self with its concomitant defensive egotism, and calmness, composure and existential security, is astonishingly apparent. Additionally, these things occur at the very foundation of the soul itself and not merely abstractly or conceptually. Indeed, to evaluate the prospect of soul metamorphosis hypothetically is utterly pointless. Its certainty is only discovered through empirical engagement. There is no contest. We eagerly engage the dispositional nature that is our undeniable preference, and we unhesitatingly relinquish our former, redundant mentality. Thereby, through an increasing vulnerability towards the supernal mind, we are qualitatively transformed according to ineffable design.

Thus, immediate cognition from the perspective of

51

the human ipseity teaches us about the qualitative and essential nature of phenomena. Fortified through our own direct experience we recognize the authenticity of intangible significances and the limitations of the exclusively physical perspective. Immediate concurrence with the supernal nature through open-hearted sincerity is thoroughly justified by our own increasing familiarity with intrinsic existence and thereby we inaugurate the inexorable dynamic of soul transformation.

The immediate cognition of the authentic condition of existence proceeds simultaneously because the perspective of divine principle reveals to us the real nature of circumstances. We discover right-mindedness and upon that basis we recognize and relinquish our specious sense of existence along with our superficial opinion of others and of circumstances. Thereby we find that our mental and emotional constitution is steadily transposed according to supernal mandate.

10. The Emancipation of the Human Heart

It would be helpful if these matters could be openly discussed and presented without being obscured by arcane, religious idiom and enigmatic, occult ambiguity. The prospect of remaining circumscribed within an egocentric mentality is not a realistic, continuing option and anything that hinders clear understanding works against us.

The transformative reorientation of the soul is essential to human progress because otherwise we will descend steadily towards an animalian status because there is no other direction to pursue. This appalling alternative needs to be clearly stated. We no longer possess the leisure to indulge the acceptable madness that passes for normality because the consequences of a continued, self-first mindset are escalating towards a critical juncture of interpersonal conflict and the disintegration of social conscience.

Selfishness is a degeneration of character whereby each seeks their own interest irrespective of the well-being of others. Furthermore, avarice becomes steadily augmented by cunning and malice, and human culture impetuously devolves into barbaric savagery.

This seemingly bleak depiction is derived not merely from the lamentable condition of human affairs throughout the world whereby callous conduct has become a tolerable norm, but through a careful scrutiny of the implications of a future condition of soul founded upon egotism. While egotism may seemingly masquerade as individuality, in fact it is an unprofitable orientation from the perspective of the health of the mind and the beneficial development humankind. Egotism is from every rational perspective a counterproductive human disposition.

However, once the essential significance of things becomes evident, we realize that the further qualitative development of the soul is of far greater significance than mere personal advantage over others. From the viewpoint of substantive progress, we begin to recognize the way things really are, and we discover the dimensional significance of the human biography. Thereupon, we find that the mentality of self-first has no place in the qualitative advancement of the human soul, and through the narrow perspective of self-centeredness, the subsequent degradation of character works against the higher interest of dispositional maturation.

It is a plain choice between intrinsic value and superficiality. Knowledge through direct encounter presents conclusive intelligence concerning the intrinsic nature of things and rouses further interest particularly when insight is qualitatively compared to conventional intelligence.

Consequently, we see how the present characteristic tenor of the human soul must become superseded by an opposite dispositional perspective. But a successive nature of sufficient worthiness cannot be adequately conceived within the human imagination. Therefore, the necessity of a complete reorientation places the necessity of an essential reconstitution beyond human, intellectual aptitude.

If we imagine that we can transform the condition of the human psyche through our own ingenuity, then we have failed to reckon with self-preservation and myriad similar inhibitions that foster egotism. Those features that pertain to self-priority are not easily dislodged because the superficial context wherein we imagine we reside, ensures that our anxiety is fully justified. Furthermore, it would be reckless to neglect our conservation through an assumed altruism or contrived morality.

Ego-centrism, as a redundant mentality is resolved through immediate communion with the supernal exemplar within the heart-of-the-soul. When the process is initiated upon the discovery of a successive principle within the heart, the development of the soul continues towards that end. Indeed, our attention becomes henceforth coordinated according to the new priority of the qualitative conversion of the human mind.

Thus, we have the measure of what constitutes significancy in terms of the human plight, and the precedence that openhearted sincerity towards the supernal must assume if we take the qualitative development of the human being at all seriously. We find that our straightforward concurrence within the crux of the human heart is at this time above any other in human history, of foremost concern.

Furthermore, the changes that we increasingly discern will convince us of the efficacy of the dynamic of soul transformation through supernal influence. Our immediate task is to make the psyche vulnerable to amelioration and to proceed with the utmost sincerity.

11. The Condition of Reality

Experience through the aegis of immediate cognition permits an encounter with the essential significance of ourselves, other people and phenomena. Only ipseity is capable of direct engagement because only the human entity itself is capable of straightforward interaction. The intellect is an intermediary faculty of the human constitution without intrinsic and individual distinction. Consequently, reason and deduction will always remain oblique and circuitous, evaluative faculties.

The human, intangible identity is able to conclusively evaluate the merit of a hypothetical interpretation of existence because it exists essentially in correspondence with the intrinsic significance of all other things. It is the ultimate statement of certainty against which human speculation concerning the nature of reality may be tried for its substance and authenticity.

The human essential is able to distinguish between a circumstantial appraisal and ultimate authenticity because there is nothing of greater certainty in our experience than our own ipseity. When we directly encounter our particular, existential significance, the reality of our own being becomes the qualitative barometer of authenticity. The direct engagement of our own existence and the immediate recognition of all other things for their elemental distinction serves as a benchmark of authenticity against which the value of human philosophy is conclusively tried. Similarly, that which we recognize as the intrinsic distinction of something or the conceptual origin of organization, is certain because it is engaged immediately through our own singular ipseity and therefore serves us conclusively as a standard of reality.

The condition wherein the intrinsic significance of things is found is not spatial but pervasive. We are familiar with physical space, and consequently the concept of essential existence is unexpected and seems obscure. But through immediate engagement we discover our own innate distinction and we find that it is not spatially circumscribed but it exists emphatically. Similarly, from the perspective of the human essence, an object of interest is encountered directly, and its essential significance is discovered to exist immanently. However, it is the immanent nature of the intrinsic proportion of things that is dismissed by conventional, materialistic exclusivity.

Normally we almost entirely emphasize the predominantly physical and obvious aspects of phenomena. Consequently, Western philosophy is particularly biased in favor of the spatially evident but otherwise superficial appearance of things. We exclude the qualitative and intrinsic dimensions from our appraisal of existence because we are unable to conclusively verify their reality in material terms. The criterion that we inevitably apply in order to determine whether an occurrence possesses existential legitimacy, is the physical condition. Without physical representation, the existence of a thing is deemed to be uncertain because we find that we do not possess the cognitive ability to conclusively evaluate the merit of phenomena that do not possess material manifestation.

But through direct engagement, the human

essence experientially enters into a straightforward encounter with the material appearance of a thing and thereby discovers the incorporeal significance of its existence. It finds a vast dimension of meaning beyond the spatial and recognizes a state wherein everything intangible exists contiguously, regardless of physical space.

Immediate cognition is an inherent, human cognitive ability that rests upon the significance of the essential distinction of the individual. Individuality, however, does not imply egotism which is an aberrant feature of the contemporary soul, but it refers to human, singular uniqueness. Through immediate engagement, the intangible existence of the intrinsic dimension of things is discovered, including the nature of human ipseity. The human essence, by direct encounter recognizes that the intangible merit of a phenomenon epitomizes the worthwhile and meaningful dimension of its existence. It is the value, qualitative significance, elemental identity, and the conceptual origin of things that is their consequential basis, and consequently immediate cognition of the overlooked, intangible magnitude is also a direct experience of reality.

Conventionally, we emphasize the material appearance and physical structure of things at the expense of the intrinsic value. We assume that the obvious condition is the full extent of the existence of phenomena. But our preoccupation with the physical is near-sighted and, consequently, we consistently fail to find meaning in the apparent and superficial because physical conditions of themselves do not possess intrinsic significance. There is nothing of perennial consequence within the transient condition of things. Physical properties alone belie intrinsic importance and essential identity, and consequently we fail to discover what something substantively is merely from a scrutiny of its conspicuous, material condition.

Very occasionally, through caprice, we may spontaneously glimpse the full dimensionality of phenomena. It is an exhilarating moment of revelation. But we quickly revert to our familiar, materialistic mentality and the momentary glance dissolves to be conveniently explained away as a neurological anomaly. In fact our brief exposure was in all likelihood the consequence of impromptu, immediate cognition through the human ipseity. What we experienced was not only the full dimensionality of a situation but the authentic condition of existence itself.

For example, if we directly engage an organic system such as a plant or creature, we discover a conceptual structure that is elusive to the scrutiny of even the microscopic, cellular composition. Convinced of the exclusive significance of the material condition of things, the conceptual incentive that propels an organism through constant dissolution and metamorphic reappearance, remains obscured from sight.

Similarly, greater than the casual recognition of a color and the vain, materialistic attempt to reduce it into quantifiable terms, the intrinsic identity exists as a particular, unique and consistent distinction wherever the particular value of coloration should arise. Likewise, a Native Element Mineral is conventionally classified by its physical properties while the inherent significance that epitomizes its elemental identity is disdained by materialistic myopia because it is thought to be merely subjectively derived and illusive. But these profound, intrinsic identities indicate an excluded magnitude of poignant relevance that is direct evidence of the meaningful dimension of existence that we recognize through immediate cognition as reality.

12. The Necessary Demise of Egotism

The lamentable condition of the human soul founded upon a psychology of egocentricity fails to be existentially meaningful because we place all our confidence in a false, personal identity and erroneous sense of detached singularity. If we recognize the need for a fundamental transformation whereby the beggarly sense of self is replaced by a stature and character beyond our own contrivance and affected merit then the vague and muddled approach towards redemption, compounded through myriad, human distortions over the centuries, is found to be clearly inadequate.

The authentic identity of the human being is the singular distinction that essentially differentiates one person from another. The petty sense of self, through its persistent uncertainty and assumed grandiosity, hinders the recognition and the establishment of the sovereignty of the human ipseity. But it is unable to transform itself because we do not possess the capacity of self-amelioration. The only possible way in which egotism is redressed is through the establishment of a disposition of willingness whereby we position our fragile sense of identity directly in the way of the immanent presence.

The heart, as the locus of the affections is necessarily unsophisticated and susceptible. Open-hearted sincerity is the only viable approach towards the immanent presence because it is the human psyche itself that requires reorientation. An entirely different basis than egocentricity is essential and, consequently, the soul must be rendered vulnerably to the direct influence of the ideal principle.

Clearly, an imperious, self-important stance makes a mockery of the dynamic of soul metamorphosis. Yet, frequently, the sanctimonious will implore and cajoled deity for favor in the manner of the devotee of a supernatural despot, that has to be seduced in order to serve humanity. As long as the transformation of the soul is obscured and confused through superstition and dogma, human progress inevitably remains beleaguered. If we imagine that we can maintain our obsolete self-centered mentality and simultaneously become reoriented towards decency, probity and altruism, we have thoroughly misunderstood the significance and consequence of the transformational dynamic of our essential nature. Our ambiguous expectations will run contrary to reality because their basis is fabricated.

Egotism is the central malaise of the human psyche. It is neither replaced nor commuted by our own effort because egocentricity cannot commute itself. The false sense of self becomes reoriented through the immediate experience of supernal goodwill and amity. This does not somehow occur externally through liturgy or ritual but it requires that the affections be rendered susceptible to the immanent presence through scrupulous sincerity. There is no value in a disinterested, mechanical formality as if the consequence of certain, repetitious observances ensured the establishment of our authentic identity.

The central condition of the human constitution needs to be newly established upon existential confidence instead of a self-centered misidentification. The human ipseity is our authentic identity and selfishness has no part in it. The transformation from egocentricity is achieved through the strategic disposal of the psyche towards the transformative influence of the immanent presence. A doubtful and precariously established psyche that relies upon its own insubstantial sense of self, is eclipsed through the certainty of divine goodwill and amity and by the immediate and intimate experience of those qualities at its foundation. Egotism is rendered moot through the immediate experience of reality revealed to the heart by the immanent presence.

Thereby, the human ipseity, that is the authentic and constant identity of the human being, begins to assume its sovereign position. It is no longer obscured through the antics of a moribund psyche that seeks reassurance through self-indulgence or by the adoption of an assumed identity that disguises its own frailty. It is this little sense of self that is ameliorated through the exemplary nature at the most profound level of our psychological establishment. The capricious and selfish pretentiousness of the egotistical self is superseded by certainty to the degree that the human psyche establishes a profound and willing concurrence with the ethos of virtue.

Disenchanted with egotism, we willingly permit the transformation of our faulty and vain sense of identity. Thereby, seemliness and integrity become positioned as the foundation of our soul in order that the human ipseity may be established as our sovereign identity. Subsequently, we readily apprehend the intrinsic nature of things and discover the full dimensionality of their existence without the hindrance of an egocentric mentality that is preoccupied with its own status.

As we progress, we discover the human, authentic

identity through immediate cognition and our position is found to be existentially secure because the soul becomes reestablished upon the certainty of immediacy and permanence.

The human ipseity exists within an immanent concurrence with the supernal and becomes positioned within the human constitution as the absolute existential certitude of our existence. But the process of metamorphic transformation remains incomplete until we consistently identify with the nature of the immanent presence within the core of our soul and allow our egotistical misidentification to become transmuted. Within the fabric of human existence, the contingency of a psychological transformation is instituted whereby the erroneously established condition of self-centeredness may be ameliorated through the immediacy of divine goodwill. Thus, the immanent presence exposes us the to the authentic state and structure of our intrinsic constitution.

The desire to identify with the graciousness and goodwill of the supernal nature is facilitated by a predilection and affection that supersedes egotism. Immediate concurrence requires open-hearted sincerity and concomitant vulnerability, but nothing more. Subsequently, through immediate engagement, the human soul is qualitatively reproduced after an archetypal ideal of propriety and rectitude.

While we immediately experience the presence of goodwill and amity through open-hearted sincerity, yet we do not need to attempt self-amelioration and the correction of our disposition. Direct and intimate exposure to the quality and nature of the supernal

66

exemplar captivates the heart and through profound affection we desire to adopt graciousness and dignity as our own nature, which is in actuality, our authentic, essential condition.

The petty, segregated sense of self is established upon a distorted perception that is a result of our failure to apprehend the authentic condition of things. That essential significance, that we fail to discover through an exclusively materialistic view-point, we similarly overlook in terms of our own constitution. Conventionally, we assume that the superficial appearance of things represents the entire existence of phenomena. Similarly, we imagine that our identity is circumscribed by our fragile ego. But we cannot simultaneously identify with a counterfeit identity of egotism while endorsing our authentic status and therein lies the dynamic necessity of our supernal reestablishment.

The psychological malaise of egocentricity is eclipsed through an immediate association with the exemplary nature because the essential conditions of existence are revealed to us at a foundational level. Whenever we recognize a reversion to our former self-centeredness, we synchronize with immanent goodwill and our perspective is transformed.

Thereby, we increasingly engage phenomena and circumstances from the perspective of the human ipseity which improvement further reinforces our determination to the task before us and allows our egotistical nature to be transformed into propriety and decency. We have glimpsed how things exist in their fullness, and we are loath to revert to our former myopia. Thereafter, there is no substitute for reality that we could possible entertain.

13. Forgiveness

Only the egotistical sense of self is preoccupied with resentment. The ipseity is existentially secure and recognizes its own unique and intransient distinction and that of others. But the counterfeit identity is beset by conservational anxiety. It is easily roused and inevitably defensive. It seeks to preserve a semblance of relevance because it assumes that it is unworthy and mortally composed, and it is fearful through knowledge of its vulnerability. In other words, resentment arises through profoundly established misperception in terms of existential significance and individual inadequacy.

Once the human ipseity is recognized through immediate cognition as the sovereign identity of the human constitution, the need to sustain and bolster the counterfeit representation would seem superfluous. But the subliminal status of a discordant psyche is not so easily dislodged. While it would appear that defensiveness and self-preservation should be easily recognized as futile in the light of the experiential recognition of the human, authentic identity, the egocentric disposition lingers on because it is established within the crux of the feeling nature itself.

Consequently, it is within the human soul that the disparity must be addressed. If we could assure the egotistically oriented, human psyche that it no longer requires consolation and gratification then the task of transformation from a small and existentially uncertain sense of self, to the immediate recognition of ipseity would be complete.

But if the psyche were to attempt the self-amelioration of its own existential ambivalence it would lead to a bewildering contradiction because the conviction of vulnerability is basally established and beyond the reach of reason.

Thus, we recognize the necessity of an intervention within the central substance of the human soul. This is only successfully attained through the agency of conciliation within the human heart. For this purpose, the medium of reorientation is the presence of caritas and benignity that reassures the soul through the immediate experience of the supernal nature and thereby dissolves existential anxiety and attendant defensiveness. Through divine intervention at the most profound level of the human constitution, the human heart intimately identifies with the successive nature as if it were its own. Thereupon, the soul relinquishes subjective concern and is able to embrace its authentic status without antagonism.

The transformation of human egotism is not a small task because we quickly discover that any essential confrontation to our insecure disposition, even on our own part, is met with vicious resistance. Any attempt to remonstrate with the solitary sense of self is inevitably received as a challenge to its existence and therein lies the poignancy and deadlocked predicament of the contemporary, human condition.

We are defensively oriented, but the essential assurance of the presence of goodwill and amity allows us to relinquish egotism and we discover, to the contrary, that vulnerability is not fatal. At the moment that we turn to the endorsement of the immanent presence, our perspective alters from anxious subjectivity, and we permit the human affections to be reoriented after the divine Ideal. Thereupon, we recognize that vulnerability is a crucial precondition to the qualitative improvement of the human soul, and that within a receptive heart there is no danger because through supernal goodwill and amity we find ourselves at liberty to relinquish anxiety. Every time we sense a dissonance arising within our psyche; we turn the attention of our heart towards the immanent presence and our defensive stance becomes steadily and gladly ameliorated.

Clearly, the disparity between individual circumstances is enormous. The one person may not recognize an urgent of further improvement and casually postpone the qualitative advancement of the soul because the circumstances do not seem pressing. Another may be in dire standing but fail to recognize that a vulnerable constitution is opportune and not disadvantageous.

However, the optimum approach arises from the recognition that the conventional, human condition consists of cognitive and existential bondage. Consequently, we assist our own progress towards emancipation and autonomy if we acknowledge that we are at a pivotal moment in time wherein meaningful, human advancement requires a metamorphic transformation. An impersonal review of the individual mentality reveals that the need is not discretionary but critical.

Therefore, susceptibility towards the agencies of reconstruction would seem a very slight contribution when we consider the potential advantage. We move from subjectivity to vulnerability through the immediate assurance of goodwill and amity. The task is straightforward because we do not need to accomplish magnanimity but we experience it directly through open-hearted sincerity.

Through openhearted sincerity, those things that provoke defensiveness, and by disquiet, impede the recognition and establishment of the human ipseity as our sovereign identity, are acknowledged and unmasked. Vulnerability replaces defensiveness and, through the aegis of the goodwill of the immanent presence, resentment and bitterness towards others are appropriately viewed from the reference of existential security. We willingly absolve others because our view-point is reestablished upon a position of certainty wherein we no longer feel compelled to safeguard a false sense of self.

Having unequivocally released others through the aegis of the magnanimity that replaces our defensive psyche upon a sound footing, we find that our own transgressions become similarly mitigated, and we yearn to make amends in whatever manner seems appropriate, judicious and prudent. Yet, significantly, the alteration of our perspective from resentment to goodwill may be the most important strategy, while the value of remorse is to further induce determination and resolve to continue our own development. For the rest, some things cannot be set right and very gladly and courageously we leave them to providence, secure in the certainty of divine goodwill towards all, through our own immediate and intimate experience.

14. The Straightforward Approach

In spite of the episcopal insistence of superior acumen and status, there is no substitute expertise or surrogate representation that can take the place of our own direct encounter with the supernal. The hierarchy of priestly government that pretends a superior authority over our own directly ascertained knowledge, is merely a humanly fabricated caste, valuable in a general sense but otherwise irrelevant to the actual circumstances of soul transformation.

The profound task of soul transformation consists of an intimate communion solely concerning the individual and the immanent presence. Accordingly, the implication of an exclusive brokerage between an ecclesiastical authority and divinity obscures individual progress if it assumes precedence over our own straightforward engagement. No one can serve as an intermediary and the suggestion that a congregation is assured a special dispensation through elite leadership is merely political in its purpose and embarrassing in its assumption.

We enter the immediate presence and discover supernal goodwill and amity through the aegis of our own approach of open-hearted sincerity. If we are insincere, communion cannot take place. We only engage the supernal upon terms of ingenuousness whereby forthrightness supersedes conceptual preparedness or advanced theological knowledge.

Religious authority notwithstanding, even the neurologist will inform us that our immediate experience of the exemplary nature is no more than a brain anomaly.

We find this an extraordinary interpretation particularly because the encounter between ourselves and the immanent presence occurs through the heart and not the cerebellum. In other words the psyche is in accessible through the human body or through any of its faculties.

It is unfortunate that the dynamics of soul transformation are obscured by the narrow view of the medical specialist and through human misconstruction. It is as if the metamorphosis of the soul were a mere belief or a mental excess in the manner of euphoria. Unhappily, that which is profoundly significant towards further human development is thereby maligned not through actual knowledge of the subject but by inherent prejudice. Thereby, something vitally significant is demeaned to be peculiarly emotional and further ridiculed as merely superstition or make-believe.

Yet, the extravagant elaboration and hyperbole of something that is plainly practical, inevitably obscure the original intent. The non-invested onlooker merely recognizes human chicanery and deception because the central purpose appears enigmatic and contradictory. Consequently, through predispositional bias we fail to distinguish the existence of the inherent, transformational dynamic that is pivotal to human advancement.

We do not know the nature of the immanent presence except partly and gradually through immediate, open-hearted engagement. Therefore, it is pointless to attempt a definition. Similarly, a significant hindrance to the practice of direct cognition through the perspective of the human ipseity, lies in the assumption of knowledge and the grafting of our own interpretation upon unknown things prior to significant, empirical inquiry.

It is entirely the same when we encounter the immanent presence through open-hearted sincerity. It works entirely against our own interest to assume prior intelligence because we thereby obscure the straightforward encounter and open ourselves to all manner of ambiguity and pretense. Furthermore, pretense is derivative of egocentricity which is the obsolete condition of soul that we hope and desire to overcome.

We embark upon an essential, transformational progression through the dual accedence of prior ignorance concerning the nature of the immanent presence and anticipation of a newly transformed disposition and perspective at the conclusion of the metamorphic process. While through immediate cognition of the human ipseity we discover the nature of our authentic distinction and thereby recognize the quality towards which we aspire, it is through innocence and vulnerability towards the goodwill and amity of the supernal that the transmutation of the human psyche is assured.

Innocence and simplicity are the prerequisite attitudinal approach towards divine goodwill otherwise the heart remains inaccessible to supernal ingress. But ingenuousness may be inappropriate in relation to the world. Simplicity is readily misconstrued as credulity and foolishness. Furthermore, it is counterproductive to be gullible in human affairs because they are predominantly driven by self-interest and not necessarily fairness. However, the gradual demise of egocentricity through open-hearted sincerity towards the immanent presence is replaced not with silliness but with wisdom and judgment founded upon perspective and through direct knowledge and insight.

The transformation of the psyche from self-centeredness to existential certainty is not humanly achievable because it requires the immediate presence of the exemplary, supernal nature within the innermost foundation of the human psyche. Consequently, the unsophisticated and vulnerable approach is the only appropriate demeanor towards soul amelioration. For this reason, the individual task, readily applicable to every person whatever their situation or station in life, is openhearted sincerity.

These things pertaining to the further development of human kind should be explored straightforwardly in order that we do not waste our time on ineffectual practices. Through immediate cognition we recognize the full dimensionality of existence, yet while this encourages the process, such knowledge is not a prerequisite. Nevertheless, it serves us because thereby we know for ourselves what reality is like and consequently we are not easily mislead by futile misdirection.

15. The Heart as a Cognitive Agency

Without physical evidence, the existence of pervasive goodwill as the significant agency of soul transformation remains uncertain because it implies that the source of human transformation exists as an entity. But through immediate cognition from the exclusive view-point of the human ipseity, we discover that within the intrinsic, intangible dimension of phenomena there occurs a substantial, intangible distinction. We find that the physical belies the elemental particularity, and that is of greater significance than the obvious appearance. Therefore, we discover that physical evidence alone merely reveals incomplete intelligence and that there exists a far more profound and more meaningful magnitude than that indicated by the material structure.

Those who are convinced that existence is composed solely of the physical status of things will inevitably remain unpersuaded perhaps even in the face of their own experiences to the contrary. The material condition is easy to confirm and, consequently, tangible attestation overrides experiential cognition because subjectively derived knowledge is impossible to handle and manipulate in physical terms. Therefore, the materialist remains preoccupied with the superficial, unable to appreciate that elemental significances are both intangible and thoroughly characteristic.

We cannot discover something formerly unknown to us if we determinedly maintain a conceptual opinion and thereby commence our investigations from a partisan position. Experientially, intangible significances are conclusively recognized as specific and not mere anonymous forces. Although they cannot be managed in the manner of physical evidence, to deny their existence is only possible in the abstract.

The intangible dimension of material conditions is indiscernible from an exclusively, physically perceptible view-point. Through original and unprejudiced, immediate cognition we discover inherent value and thereby the greater, incorporeal magnitude and inherent significance of phenomena.

Failing the discovery and development of the practice of immediate cognition, and subsequently the recognition of the human ipseity as our sovereign identity, the transformational dynamic of soul metamorphosis through open-hearted concurrence with the immanent presence, will at first be approached more from a position of trust than resting upon conclusive evidence. Nevertheless, recognizing the essential importance of the requirement of a dramatic change of disposition in order to promote further human development, a tentative and sincere, open-minded posture will quickly offer conviction and confirm the existence of the transformative dynamic.

While the direct experience of the immanent presence through open-hearted sincerity, is necessarily subjective, the steady abandonment of our egocentric and defensive mentality yields compelling results as to the efficacy of the experience. Furthermore, by determined candor and our own individual, purposeful and straightforward approach, we become increasingly unsusceptible to deception but remain highly critical of wishful thinking and misrepresentation. Ultimately, through a demeanor of impartiality and sincerity, we recognize the tenuous position of chimerical metaphysics and promptly renounce humanly contrived elaboration. Since our process is not a common belief system but concerns our own efforts and the subsequent amelioration of dispositional perspective, we remain confident.

Correspondence with the immanent presence occurs through the heart. As an anonymous function, reason is incapable of direct engagement and, consequently, intellectual evaluation is always circuitous and indirect in nature. Reason and speculation concerning soul transformation can never lead to conclusive knowledge because deduction provides only an oblique, evaluative appraisal of a situation. Intangible existence can only be known definitively through direct engagement and immediate experience because it exists in a condition of immanency. It is through the heart that the amelioration of the self-centered soul must occur because the metamorphic transformation of the psyche is personal, not objective. It is not the intellect that requires foundational amendment but the human psychology.

The human heart opens to the immanent presence, quieting the incessant opinions of the intellect and the turmoil of emotional evaluation. Through a respite of mental activity, an encounter is established with the goodwill and amity of the principle of an exemplary ethos and the dysfunctional psyche is superseded by an intimacy of immutable and unequivocal affection within the human heart.

It is the open heart that commences the concurrence and it is within the heart that the individual experiences a vastness of unambiguous beneficence. Thereby the human psyche is immutably impressed, and a transformation commences towards a far better nature.

Therefore, the individual task is to make ourselves receptive and vulnerable through open-hearted sincerity. In the sense of soul transformation, it is the heart that becomes the agency of cognition and of definite evaluation.

16. Abstractly Conceived Materialistic Philosophy

Abstract: An abstract idea is separated by the mind from the objects to which they belong or inhere. Whiteness is an abstract idea because it is conceived in the mind abstracted from snow, a wall or any other substance that is white. Qualities are abstracted from the subjects in which they are inherent. By the operation of abstraction the mind creates for itself a multitude of new ideas. English Synonyms, George Crabb (1778 – 1851).

An abstract concept never possesses actual existence while it remains separate from an extant context. Ideas without inherent pertinence may seem logical and inventive, yet they remain remote from reality by virtue of their independence from realistic implementation. Until a concept is demonstrated as authentic through practical application, it remains hypothetical. This is why a postulate cannot be conclusively demonstrated as valid through further conjecture and deduction until it is tried and proven to be authentic.

This is because the intellect is a calculating agency without the capacity to immediately engage a situation and discover conclusive testimony concerning its existence. Rationale cannot test a hypothesis: it can merely compound the speculative.

We cannot reason the validity of something whose existence is constitutionally unamenable to physical representation because the deduction of physically remote conditions will inevitably rests upon insubstantial evidence. Therefore, is futile to debate the authenticity of a situation that must be directly experienced in order to be known unless a person has first-hand knowledge concerning those circumstances. That is to say, abstract evaluation is incommensurate with immediately ascertained knowledge and will inevitably struggle to accommodate intangible information.

Consequently, those who possess scholarship without a foundation of empirically validated knowledge are not in a position to evaluate the authenticity of the existence of something that is only discerned through direct engagement. Furthermore, the authority of peer consensus is a meaningless measure when applied to the appraisal of the intangible dimension of existence because there is nothing quantifiable for the intellect to calculate. In other words, the existence of intangible evidence is not disproven upon the strength of a counter, but untried hypothesis.

Postulation without demonstrable application, irrespective of academic endorsement, is incompatible when it comes to intangible value if the exponent endeavors to reason something that is only discernible through immediate engagement.

Existential conceptualization is an oxymoron if the intellect cannot definitively identify the nature of intangible significances and if the meaningful dimension of existence is not materially apparent. Unless the approach concerning the verification of essential, intangible existence or its disavowal, rests upon actual experience, it remains meaningless. In other words, the intrinsic value of things is found solely through immediate cognition, and it may only be successfully evaluated upon those terms.

Immediate cognition capacitates the direct engagement of a phenomenon in the context of its actual existence. The human ipseity does not calculate but encounters circumstances immediately. Furthermore, as an entity, the human being is able to experience phenomena directly, but the physical brain endeavors to obliquely appraise and consider what something based upon indirectly acquired information.

The human body is not an entity, and consequently the biological organs cannot experience the intrinsic significant of something. Only the human ipseity is able to encounter phenomena and circumstances without intermediary assessment.

The intellect always functions indirectly because it does not, of itself, possess being. Materialistic, Western philosophy supposes that the body and its functions comprise the full extent of human existence. But this simplistic and abstract opinion is negated through immediate cognition. Thereby, the individual entity discovers its own uniqueness and singularity from which perspective a vast dimension of meaningfulness unfolds that is otherwise physically negligible.

To stress once again, the existence of intangible significances may be assessed only speculatively by means of intellectual postulation. In which case, the authentication or the negation of intrinsic distinction can never be conclusively justified through deduction.

In order to offer reliable findings, the reasoning faculties must appraise what something is from compatible evidence. Otherwise, incongruous information will need to be evaluated in other, more appropriate way. Unable to immediately encounter intangible circumstances and definitively evaluate intrinsic significances through rationale and calculation, intrinsic value is justified successfully only through immediate cognition.

Otherwise, the indirectly functioning intellect searches to determine if a proposal makes sense but in order to unequivocally assess the authenticity of something, the thinker must possess an explicit standard of authenticity of a similar nature as that of the object under question. Unfortunately, the convenient benchmark of the materialistic naysayer is merely established upon partiality or unrelated information, but not through immediate engagement. Consequently, judgment is passed concerning the significance of intangible existence, without appropriately qualified authority.

In other words, if we identify the human, intrinsic significance merely with the body, then we inevitably remain superficially preoccupied within physical parameters. From such a perspective we cannot realistically appraise physically elusive, incorporeal conditions.

A perspective towards existence that predetermines exclusively physical characteristics and the obvious properties of phenomena to be the full dimension of their existence, is derived from abstract speculation and not from empirical cognition. However, immediate experience reveals the intangible evidence of a vast volume of significance, and even if it is introspectively garnered, only immediate cognition offers a truly consonant approach towards its evaluation.

However, those who rightly abhor superstition and irrationality may take heart. Immediate cognition is a thoroughly disciplined process of discernment that does not negate the existence of the physical but qualifies the shallow view with more profound meaning. Through the direct engagement of things we discover more than the material proportion, but thereby we identify the existential qualification and intrinsic value that pertains to a more profound, essential significance.

The philosophical denial of the existence of the intangible significances of physical appearances contradicts common experience. Yet, abstractly conceived, materialistic exclusivity remains an acceptable Western philosophical position with disastrous consequences for meaningful, human advancement.

The problem is that the materialist from a position of philosophical prejudice, dismisses the essential value and intrinsic, qualitative significances of physical phenomena, and the implication of the existence of the innate meaningfulness of things, to the detriment of a more complete understanding of life. Even though to deny essential existence in practice is absurd, all metaphysical circumstances are similarly discarded with categorical discrimination. Thereby, upon the authority of the abstract philosopher, we come to believe that we are merely mortal and solely, physically circumscribed. Thus, abstractly conceived, materialistic, Western philosophy, for all the rationalistic erudition that appears to support the shallow view, remains only an abstract postulation alike to any other, that does not stand up in practice.

17. Probity, Dignity and Stature

That which is lacking from the development and establishment of a wholesome disposition and concomitant future is the practical transformation of the human psyche. All our other efforts are negated because of the obsolescence of a self-centered and impoverished mindset. Our plight is that we are unable to effectively transform our mentality and demeanor because the means to do so have become confused and obscured. We may imagine that we may forcefully improve our own psychology through discipline, affirmation or meditation but in reality, we cannot because the psyche, unlike the body, is not susceptible to self-amelioration because character is basally entrenched and deeply conditioned.

While behavioral change may seem advantageous, nevertheless, improvement remains provisional and our efforts must be constantly extended. Unfortunately, the probity required in order to advance towards a meaningful, human future is unattainable through even the most stringent discipline. Yet, the accomplishment of a substantive destiny requires the absolute transformation of the human heart and its restitution upon an opposite foundation.

Recognition of the incorporeal ipseity and its establishment as the sovereign view-point and individual distinction of the human being, is the foundation of immediate cognition. We are tremendously influenced by the realization and experience of human singularity and by the intrinsic nature of the knowledge derived through direct encounter. But a moribund mentality will always provoke conflict and procrastination.

Unfortunately, the necessity of a preliminary, ethical transformation before the undertaking of metaphysical understanding, is entirely understated because we assume that a mere adjustment in behavior will suffice. We fail to realize that our obsolete mentality must be superseded by a disposition of incomprehensible dignity and stature in order that the soul may qualitatively progress. Meanwhile, our confused attempts towards morality more frequently resemble self-righteousness and Puritanism than integrity.

The solution to this dilemma does not reside within the human constitution, and it is unattainable through our own abilities. Nevertheless, there exists an agency contiguous to the human heart but externally positioned from the moribund human psyche, that possesses the necessary transformative qualification.

The paradox of externality and immanence, rests upon the nature of intrinsic existence. The particular, inherent distinction of a person or thing is immanently extant. It is only the physical condition that exists spatially. While the essential is immediately apprehended through immediate cognition, the distinction between the intrinsic distinctions of phenomena occur characteristically in the form of qualitative differentiation.

Conversant almost exclusively with material conditions, we are unfamiliar with immediacy although we recognize that the essential distinction of phenomena is not adequately represented in the appearance of things. However, we readily discover the profundity of intangible value ourselves through our own direct experience, even if at first the material conditions appear to retain the greater significance.

Essential distinctions are not spatially represented, nevertheless, they exist independently. For example, the intrinsic particularity of the color red is entirely different in distinction and quality from yellow. It is through nuances of the essential quality that the fine painter recognizes the variation in distinction between the two.

Be that as it may, when we come to articulate intrinsic distinction we find ourselves hampered if the terms of description that we use are merely physical. We discover that we must apply metaphoric and figurative phrasing in order to distinguish between elemental characteristics because their essential distinction exists intangibly.

Thus, physical terminology is found to be inadequate because when we rely on physical calibration we can only approximate the measure of the qualitative value between the colors red and yellow. Furthermore, we lose the inherent distinction of the phenomenon because the reduction of a color to a numerical formula ignores the quality. In other words, spatial values are incommensurate with intrinsic significances. Only the superficial appearance of things can be quantified, quality must be directly and experientially evaluated.

Within the condition of immanent existence, the disposition of the soul evokes compatible qualitative distinctions. In this sense we enter into an immediate association alike to an animal that affiliates with a flock or herd. Therefore, the soul, encumbered with an obsolete mentality chooses to appeal to a successive disposition by immediate concurrence. Thereupon, through the resolution of open-hearted sincerity, the human soul is rendered receptively to those same virtues.

Our task is to open the heart in active receptivity. Through open-hearted sincerity we make ourselves thoroughly vulnerable towards the efficacious and consequential prominence of the immanent presence. The unaffected approach towards the benignity of virtue initiates a process of reconstruction because our immediate experience of the supernal is itself transformative. A self-perpetuating dynamic is inaugurated through an immediate encounter with the affection of unequivocal beneficence.

Against the immediately encountered supernal exemplar, our own mentality is recognized as severely impoverished and we yearn to emulate the new. Making ourselves amenable to the transformative virtue of the immanent presence, the human psyche becomes concertedly establish upon the prospective nature.

But it must be reiterated, we cannot appropriately metamorphose our own disposition and it is counterproductive to pretend to do so. In order that our progressive transformation should be flawlessly accomplished, we must allow the immanent presence to perform the conversion. Our task is to be willing and to make ourselves receptive.

The immanent presence overwhelms the human heart and thereby transforms it according to its own nature. But it is not through our own excellence or genius that these things are accomplished. The required reestablishment does not originate within the human constitution but exists in direct accessibility awaiting our willing exposure and accordance.

18. Cognitive Estrangement

Existence is a continuum and the way towards further human development resides inherently within its architecture. The transformation of the human disposition from egocentricity to altruism in order that it may be suitably reestablished in proportion to a meaningful destiny, is essential.

Through pragmatism and an increasingly exclusive emphasis upon the utilitarian amenity of things, we have become estranged from the essential value of the existence of ourselves and of phenomena. It is as if the profound and meaningful proportion were hidden from our view in order that we might become thoroughly familiar with the sensible.

Through separation and subsequent ignorance concerning the intangible consequence of things, the human heart finds itself qualitatively bereft of indispensable nourishment that is relevant and appropriate to our essential nature. We endeavor to assuage that inner poverty through superficial expedients because in our cognitively estranged condition they seem substantial to us. But to the essential human being there is no lasting sustenance in transient conditions because we are of dimensionally greater proportion than the temporal and phenomenal aspect of existence.

Furthermore, the deceptive substitution of the transient for the enduring is possible only because we mistakenly assume that the superficial possesses substantial value. All the while, complete fulfillment is immanently accessible and awaits our discovery. Forthwith, the intensity with which we have investigated

91

the physical portion of existence must now be applied towards the exploration of substantial, intangible existence because only the intrinsic merit of things possesses ultimate significance to the essential, human being.

The manner whereby the human psyche is refashioned requires that we decisively and candidly open the heart to the immanent presence of goodwill and amity. We do this instead of indulging in self-absorption and, in all likelihood upon the ruins of a long and disconcerting passage of selfishness. Thereby our nature becomes steadily transposed after the quality and distinction of our immediate experience of the supernal exemplar.

Soul transformation requires personal participation and it is unattainable by the indirect agency of intercession. Unfortunately, distorted, religious structures that fail to clearly present the dynamic of individual conversion and instead substitute an alternative, secondary approach, merely hinder human progress. If they obscure the essential pertinence of individual, dispositional transformation through the aegis of supernal influence, then they are worse than useless. They establish a counterfeit wherein conformity with a human construction becomes of a greater priority than the actual task of soul amelioration. Accordingly, we need to set aside what we imagine we know and what others tell us concerning these things and explore them straightforwardly and pragmatically for ourselves.

Caritas does not magically transform the human soul, but our immediate engagement of the immanent presence profoundly alters our disposition because it reveals an exemplary nature that is qualitatively antithetical to egotism. On the other hand, some sort of magical transfiguration would deny us our potential autonomy. Therefore, it is essential that we embrace the dynamic of change and involve ourselves directly in the election. A qualitative comparison between our own egocentricity and the exemplary principle is striking and we yearn to adopt and absorb that nature instead of our familiar condition with all its tiresome shortcomings. We increasingly come to rely upon the certainty and perspective of goodwill and amity through open-hearted concurrence and it becomes steadily established as the primary resource in all our undertakings. Instead of our former egotistical identification, we rely upon our immediate engagement with the immanent presence as our impetus and motivation.

The immanent presence is discovered through the open heart, and our concurrence is of mutual affection because we essentially identify with the divine nature. Therein lie the dynamic of our transformation. There is nothing mystical or unusual about this except that, conventionally, we assume that relevance is determined through the spatial, material properties of things and we doubt the significance of metaphysical reality. But the immanent presence is essential and does not reside superficially or peripherally but inherently and intangibly. In this manner, the supernal nature is engaged directly without material circumstances, and it exists in a readily accessible immediate condition to the sincere heart.

Essential communication is established without rote phraseology and incantation because it is a communion of complete significance and profound implication. Consequently, concurrence between the human soul and the immanent presence does not require verbal articulation but only the exchange of complete sincerity and receptivity.

Through sincere, open-hearted candor with the immanent presence and future human paradigm we are guided and counseled as to the authentic nature of things beyond their apparent significance or representation. Increasingly, we discover things as they really are.

Experienced first-hand through the aegis of goodwill and amity, we are encouraged towards a successive mentality that supersedes egotism. Through the direct influence of the supernal nature, our myopic and self-centered mentality is steadily superseded by a successive disposition. Our task is to place ourselves willingly at the expediency of the immanent presence in order that the transformation of our psyche may be facilitated while we mature and expand towards a meaningful future.

19. The Relinquishment of Self-centeredness

As earlier stated, intellectual preoccupation, whereby we supposed that through deduction we are able to discover the authentic nature of existence, is deceptive because reason is a corporeal faculty that only functions indirectly. In order to discern the intrinsic significance of something we must approach it directly and thereby we insightfully experience its inherent distinction. Consequently, definitive knowledge concerning the intangible value of phenomena is only achievable through the perspective of the human ipseity which is our sovereign identity.

In this regard, the intellect hinders the recognition of the entirety of the existence of a phenomenon if it assumes that contemplation alone is sufficiently competent and constitutes the full extent of our cognitive ability. Our narrow perspective is exacerbated by the affected status of intellectual preeminence whereby we supposed that our cerebral dexterity is sufficiently qualified to deduce the nature of essential existence or discount its reality. Oblique deliberation can never reveal intangible significances because incorporeal value must be immediately engaged in order to be recognized.

The materialistic conviction that the physical appearance of things possesses the entirety of their significance rest upon an unsound assumption. The experiential cognition of unquantifiable value is reputed to be subjective and consequently deemed to provide unreliable evidence because without physical properties it cannot be precisely managed. But that presumptuous rationale intrudes upon the intangible dimension of existence where is without authority because it is incommensurate. The evidence of exclusive materialism as a philosophical interpretation of existence is contrived because a solely deliberative approach is incommensurate with the evaluation of incorporeal existence. Thus, reason is unable to conclusively deny the existence of the insensible dimension of phenomena nor challenge its significance. It merely reveals that the intellect is ill-disposed to confirm and manipulate qualitatively apparent data.

Thus, we discern the value of the immanent presence through direct experience and even though we do not yet have the full measure of it, we recognize the authenticity of its existence.

Egotism is superseded when the human heart is established upon the supernal, exemplary nature and we become attentive to the dynamic of an intimate reorientation of perspective. We become increasingly heedful and thereby facilitate our own transformation. Subsequently, things are grasped in the condition in which they actually exist and not as we assume or imagine them to be.

Except through direct, experiential engagement, we cannot know anything concerning the metaphysical for certain. Numerical exactitude reveals the manner of the function of the intellect but calculation cannot be applied to unquantifiable values. We can only deduce value with approximation. Therefore, definitive knowledge concerning the intangible dimension of existence requires immediate engagement.

It is upon the strength of human, intellectual adroitness that we egotistically assume a grandeur that we do not possess and overlook the desperate need of psychical reestablishment. We imagine that our capacity to reason is somehow of our own inception, and we attribute its profitable functioning to personal merit. Similarly, if we possess specialized knowledge on a subject, we cannot thereby assume that we are the authors. Neither can we take credit for the natural existence of anything. Thus, we discover that self-importance is an unwarranted conceit because everything we possess exists irrespectively of our worthiness or competence.

The only thing that we convincingly possess is our own intrinsic distinction. Therefore, giving up ego-centrism is hardly a loss of significance because it is not established upon the assurance of our authentic identity but upon a counterfeit self. The adoption of the supernal nature as the foundational surrogate of our psyche is a gain of vast consequence in terms of our well-being and the eventual incorporation of the human ipseity as our sovereign autonomy. Through egotism we imagine ourselves to be of greater consequence than we are but, meanwhile, we overlook the constancy of our authentic distinction that does not require reassurance.

The transformation of the human soul from self-absorption to existential certitude and subsequent altruism only requires our willing determination. It is a source of enormous consolation and relief that we are not assigned to perform our conversion ourselves but that our destiny remains secure in vastly wiser hands.

20. Conclusion

In spite of a materialistically centered conviction to the contrary, unless we encounter phenomena from the perspective of the ipseity of our essential constitution and restrain intellectual and emotional evaluation, we fail to discover the authentic condition of the existence of things. We merely identify with an obliquely conceived interpretation or an established appraisal that is remote from reality by virtue of its indirect exposition.

We only discover the intrinsic significance of things when we encounter phenomena immediately from the view-point of our sovereign identity. If we rely upon the deductive rationale of our corporeal faculties, accumulated foreknowledge or how we imagine things to be through a feeling-sentient appraisal, we always remain with an indirectly assessed depiction that belies the intrinsic circumstances of the existence of things. Only the immediate engagement through the human ipseity enables us to conclusively discover what something actually is. Through an exclusively physical scrutiny, we learn only of the transient value of things and fail to discover the intrinsic and meaningful content.

If the extent of existence was merely the material condition of things, it would be a very grim prospect indeed. Similarly, if the extent of a person were limited by their physicality everything meaningful would be gone and only soulless superficiality would remain.

The ipseity is immaculate and intransient, but the human psyche is deceptively established. The present status of the human ethos is obsolete and louche, hindering our further advancement through an egocentric disposition founded upon existential ignorance. Essentially uncertain and cognitively restricted to an oblique and peripheral perspective towards the conditions that we encounter, we imagine that our ambiguous sense of identity and meager, corporeal capacities alone circumscribe us.

Through immediate cognition, we find that the intrinsic and meaningful proportion of phenomena is discovered to exist in an instantaneous condition of intimate relationship to the human ipseity. Similarly, through open-hearted sincerity we find that Divine goodwill and amity also exist immediately to the human soul.

It is the choice and task of the individual to discover the immanent presence and to select and identify with the Divine disposition over our lesser proclivities. Thereby, the human psyche is steadily transformed from a reactive and susceptible mentality to that complexion which we directly and intimately experience of the immanent presence. Gradually the divine disposition and mien become our established psychology as self-defensiveness is superseded through supernal assurance.

This is less daunting than it would at first appear because it must be remembered that we cannot self-ameliorate from egotism to unselfishness and moderation because it requires that existential confidence and assurance be established as the foundational premise of the human psyche.

Therefore, our task is merely to permit goodwill and amity to accomplish the reorientation of our nature. It would be dispiriting indeed if we were required to emulate virtue through our personal willpower and merit. It would be the province of only the very few. However, that is not the case. Upon the incident of openhearted sincerity, a transformative process of soul amelioration is initiated irrespectively of individual scholarship of status.

However, unless the immanent presence is directly engaged through open-hearted sincerity, nothing of significance can occur and our self-centered nature would remain intact.

Every human stance, position or approach towards existence possesses its own ambient predilection that we appropriate as our own to the degree that we find ourselves persuaded. Our identification with a specific convention permits our psyche to be influenced according to the tenets of that particular coterie. But ritual, doctrine and allegiance to a righteous assembly are unproductive unless an encounter with the immanent presence is personally and intimately established. The impetus and momentum of soul transformation is an entirely individual matter.

The transformation of the soul, through the immediate presence of the supernal nature differs essentially from congregational allegiance because it is a dynamic that is not humanly established but accomplish exclusively through divine goodwill. The necessity of open-hearted sincerity and the direct engagement of goodness is the crux and substance of the dynamic of soul transformation and therein the promise of advancement and the eventual culmination of human destiny is assured.

Self-centeredness is an obsolete mentality that is superseded by a dispositional perspective wherein we

101

find ourselves existentially secure. However, reactive ego-defensiveness becomes moot through our immediate experience of the divine presence. Thus, we recognize circumstances from an insightful and comprehensive perspective instead of from the former egocentric bias. Furthermore, in terms of human relationships, we are no longer provoked or challenged because our sense of self is securely established.

Without the former sense of isolation, we become unaffected and unpretentious, and consequently we find that the prior necessity that we felt to defend a fragile sense of self, is gone. Thus, securely established, we become wholeheartedly magnanimous towards others, which is authentic forgiveness.

Through open-hearted sincerity we discover the immediate presence and through intimate concurrence, our former existential uncertainty is superseded. Thus, an entirely uncommon morality is inaugurated because it is intimately patterned upon the benign supernal disposition that is without egotism.

It is a disposition that is qualitatively remote from Puritanism and self-righteousness because we find ourselves essentially and emotionally fulfilled. Consequently, our goodwill is unfeigned and unpretentious. Furthermore, we recognize the singular distinction of others that is the particular, human, essential distinction, and nothing obstructs the immediate cognition of their uniqueness. We discover the intrinsic significance and full dimensionality of all things whereas, formerly, we were preoccupied with only the superficial representation.

An active conscience is indicative of an innate

recognition of a standard or benchmark against which we can assess our status. However, merely thinking about the transformation of the human psyche is ineffectual. When a disconcerting situation arises and our conscience reveals a disparity between the exemplary, and inappropriateness, we must enter the immediate presence and through a receptive heart and allow the new paradigm to influence our inner life. Assured of divine goodwill we readily relinquish our troubles.

We discover the qualitative value of a future, spiritual paradigm through the direct experience of the divine presence. Obviously, this is a physically indiscernible phenomenon because intangible significances are not successfully rendered through quantification or calibrated with material precision. Thereupon, we find ourselves faced with immediate experiences that are physically elusive. But we recognize through our knowledge of essential value and the inherent distinction of physical phenomena that remain corporeally indiscreet, that the meaning and dimension of things are not materially apparent but exist intrinsically.

Thus we develop a benchmark of discernment through familiarity with qualitative yet intangible value and distinction, and we find that through the perspective of the human ipseity, there exists a vast amplitude of intangible quality that is both real and enormously significant. Indeed, everything is discovered to possess an intrinsic pertinence that is not superficially apparent.

Conscience, of itself, is not an infallible indicator of dispositional discrepancy, but the direct experience of our own destined stature establishes a measure of comparison whereupon our obsolete mentality is tried and found qualitatively wanting. Thus, our conscience reveals the discrepancy and we turn to the immediate presence in order that the new may supersede the rudimentary mentality. The immediate presence ameliorates the incongruity through direct and intimate influence and thereby our characteristic and idiosyncratic disposition is amended to the degree that we abandon our supposed authority to the supernal.

We have to be self-motivated and tractable in order to pursue the transformation of the human psyche and allow a mentality to be developed that is appropriate to destined autonomy. But the direct experience of the goodwill and amity of the immanent presence and the recognition of certain advancement towards increasing maturity, ensures our constancy. We find that our own task, in order to become introspectively secure and constructively established, is comparatively slight and we willingly open our hearts to the transformative action of divine beneficence. The ipseity as the authentic, human identity is able to become steadily positioned as our autonomous, sovereign distinction and thereupon is established existential and cognitive liberty.

Other Books by the Same Author

THE IMMANENT PRINCIPLE OF INTEGRITY AND
GOODWILL
The Integration of the Principle of Virtue within the
Human heart

THE EVOLUTIONARY IMPERATIVE OF OUR TIME
*The Crucial Establishment of an Inspired Ethos with the
Individual, Human Heart, appropriate to a Meaningful
Future*

RECONCILIATION WITH HUMAN DESTINY
*The Surrender of the Heart-of-the-Soul as the Expedient
Approach Towards Direct Engagement with the
Immanent Exemplar of a Future, Human Disposition*

THE QUALITATIVE EVOLUTION OF THE SOUL
*The Evolutionary Transformation of the Human Soul
Through Openhearted Sincerity Towards Immanent
Caritas*

THE SUPERNAL ETHOS
Unanimity with the Divine Nature

THE BEGINNING OF WISDOM
Knowledge through Immediate Engagement

UNDER THE AEGIS OF IMMANENT CARITAS
*The Reorientation of the Human, Disparate Self-
circumscribed Mentality*

107

THE DECEPTION OF MATERIALISTIC WESTERN PHILOSOPHY
An Exploration of the Physically Elusive Volume of Existence

THE MEANINGFUL VOLUME OF EXISTENCE
An Exploration of the Overlooked Intangible Significance of Phenomena

THE OBSOLETE SELF
Individual Uniqueness and Significance beyond Egocentrism

THE TRANSFORMATION OF THE SOUL
From Self-centeredness to Sovereign Autonomy

THE IMPLICATION OF HUMAN, INCORPOREAL EXISTENCE
The Overlooked Significance of the Intangible and Qualitative Dimension of Existence

IMMEDIATE EXPERIENTIAL COGNITION
The Inherent Human Capacity of Immediate Engagement

THE HUMAN ESSENTIAL IDENTITY
Direct Experience of the Intangible Significance of Existence through the Immediate Engagement of the Human Essence

KNOWLEDGE THROUGH DIRECT COGNITION
The Human Conscious Individuality and Immediately Experienced Reality